Freelance Foodcrafting

How To Become Profitably Self-Employed in Your Own Creative Cooking Business

by Janet Shown

Live Oak Publications
Boulder, Colorado

Library of Congress Cataloging in Publication Data

Shown, Janet.
    Freelance Foodcrafting.

    Bibliography: p.
    1. Cookery. 2. Home-based businesses. 3. Self-
employed. I. Title.
TX652.S535 1983   641.5'068   83-808
ISBN: 0-911781-00-5 (pbk.)

ISBN: 0-911781-00-5

Library of Congress Catalog Card Number: 83-47652

Published by   Live Oak Publications
                  P.O. Box 2193
                  Boulder, CO 80306

Table of Contents

Chapter 1
Opportunities in Foodcrafting

America is in the midst of a culinary revolution, and there's never been a better time than now to profit from cooking. Never before has America witnessed such a surge of interest in new, exciting tastes. Consumers are snapping up such delicacies as Bulgarian caviar, fresh truffles, goat cheese, raspberry mousse, and brandied fruit in quantities that astound industry analysts, all the while pouring millions of dollars into the coffers of imaginative cooks who create and sell such food. Gourmet and specialty foods and their preparation have become so popular that *Food & Wine Magazine* dubbed the 1980s the "decade of the gourmet."

Evidence of America's gourmet food binge is everywhere. Metropolitan department stores are rapidly developing large specialty food sections, and cooking classes are popping up even in rural areas around the country.

Gourmet and specialty food businesses, both large and small, are thriving on the new food consciousness. On the small side is Les Trois Petits Cochons, founded in 1976 with $14,000. The Manhattan charcuterie's sales hit $2 million in 1982 as its owners shipped 600,000 pounds of pate to gourmet shops around the country. On the large side is Byerly's, the nation's largest gourmet food chain. With plush carpeting, crystal chandeliers and high-priced fancy foods, the six-store chain pulled in $125 million that same year.

Direct-mail food sales, once a small market limited to a few smoked hams and Christmas fruitcakes, now total upwards of $550 million a year. Retail sales have hit record highs and are expected to peak at $6.2 billion in 1990, according to Frost & Sullivan, a New York marketing research firm. Newspapers are rapidly expanding their food sections, and subscriptions to magazines like *Gourmet, Bon Appetit* and *Food & Wine* have doubled, tripled, and even quadrupled in recent years, making them some of the nation's fastest growing publications. Even Sears has entered the lucrative gourmet food field, offering 14 pages of specialty food items in a recent Christmas catalog.

Causes of the Gourmet Food Boom

Food experts disagree on a definition of gourmet foods, but Frost & Sullivan reports that these elements are usually evident: exoticism, a lack of common availablility, relatively high prices, uniqueness, and more human involvement with the processing or creation of the products. Typical gourmet shoppers, according to the report, are between the ages of 25 and 44 with a household income of $30,000 or more. They are well educated, sophisticated, and pay considerable attention to the healthfulness, quality, and status of their lives.

A confluence of forces is responsible for the tremendous popularity that gourmet and specialty foods currently enjoy. American soldiers stationed in Europe after World War II discovered delicious cuisines and a much greater appreciation of the finer points of food preparation than was common at home. Returning to the States, they searched for comparable foods in restaurants and sought the ingredients for preparing European cuisines at home. In the decades that followed, education, affluence, and travel all increased dramatically in the average American household, contributing to the increasing awareness of the enjoyment possible from fine foods masterfully prepared.

Demographics are also contributing to the growing demand for gourmet and specialty foods. American households have dramatically decreased in size, and there has been a huge growth in the number of one-person households. Those living in small households often feel it's not worthwhile to do much cooking at home, but quickly tire of the monotony of standard restaurant meals. And, with more than half of all married women now working outside the home, there is less time to spend in the kitchen and more money to spend on specialty and gourmet foods, especially those that are precooked and ready to serve.

Another demographic factor has to do with the baby boom. As Tom Thompson, owner of C'est Croissant, a take-out and mail-order bakery in Allentown, Pennsylvania put it, "The baby boom era has come of age." Used to a higher standard of living than their parents, baby boomers see gourmet food as an accessible luxury, one they can afford even in recession times. "People feel, 'Why settle for second best?' They'll deny a lot, they'll eat hamburger instead of steak, but the true pleasantries they still go for."

A Frost & Sullivan report confirms Tom's observations. Age and sex, according to the report, dramatically affect the foods people buy. Younger people appear to be more concerned with freshness, healthfulness, and apparent quality. In fact, 39 percent of the shoppers surveyed considered such factors as uniqueness, newness, sensory appeal, and quality to be more important than price. The current recession, instead of dampening interest in gourmet food, has actually spurred sales. As economic hardships affect American households, there is a tendency to look for more satisfaction in the simple pleasures of life. And one of those simple (and affordable) pleasures is fine food.

Also contributing to the increased demand for gourmet and specialty foods is the current widespread interest in health and fitness. Concerned about too much salt, sugar, cholesterol and chemical additives in their diets, people of all ages are turning to fresher, lighter, healthier foods.

Together with the new interest in more healthful eating is an increased interest in new and different cuisines. At the top of the list are Italian, Mexican, and Chinese foods, and a fast-rising new star, American Cuisine. The Chicago-based Market Research Corporation of America published figures in 1981 showing that in-home ethnic food consumption had risen 47 percent since 1972, and market analysts predict the trend will continue as familiarity with different cuisines grows.

Along with the new awareness of healthful and tasteful eating, brought about largely by increased media exposure and world travel, Americans are coming to view the preparation and serving of food as an enjoyable, creative pastime. People want to learn how to use the interesting new ingredients they find in supermarkets, health food stores and gourmet shops in the dishes they make at home. They spend more time testing out new foods, whether they cook them in their own kitchen or buy them from specialty shops and takeout stores. And the increasing interest in food is not limited to women—more and more men are finding that cooking can be a relaxing outlet for creative expression.

New Opportunities Created by New Interest in Food

Clearly an upheaval is taking place in the way Americans view eating and the preparation and serving of food. The culinary revolution that's taking place has received a great deal of media coverage and is widely recognized as one of the major changes in our society in recent years.

Much less widely recognized are the opportunities that have been created by these changes. Many gourmet and specialty foods require much greater quality control than is possible in large, traditional food manufacturing plants, but these foods are often ideally suited for small-scale "cottage industry" production. And since many gourmet and specialty foods are made without preservatives and depend on freshness for their superior flavor, small-scale local production is absolutely essential.

The increasing interest in food education, including preparation tips, recipes, and full cuisine instruction has opened the doors wide for cooking school teachers, food writers, and media chefs. Caterers can cash in on the growth in home and corporate entertaining, and take-out stores are only beginning to recognize their potential for sales to working men and women, picnikers, party guests, and consumers on the run. The mail-order food business can only grow as consumers seek out ethnic and gourmet foods, for even when such foods are available in retail outlets many people prefer the convenience of ordering from home.

There is a wide range of opportunities in independent foodcrafting, and anyone who loves working creatively with food should be able to find an opportunity that appeals to him. Restaurant operations are the one type of foodcrafting opportunity conspicuously missing from this book. Although many people dream of someday opening a charming little restaurant, we feel that most people would be better off at least starting with one of the other foodcrafting ventures covered in this book. Although beginners can be successful in restaurant operations, there is generally greater risk involved. A fairly substantial investment is almost invariably required, and it is extremely difficult to start and run a restaurant with less than a full-time commitment from the very beginning.

Freelance Foodcrafting Defined

In medieval times, a knight who claimed no permanent allegiance to a lord but hired himself out to the highest paying warlord was called a free lance. Down through the years, "freelance" came to describe writers, artists, researchers, and others who worked independently for those who requested their services. Because independence is the outstanding characteristic of so many of the cooking professionals profiled in this book, it's only natural to think of them as freelance cooks. But "cooks" isn't quite right, either. Although some people interviewed do, indeed, make their living by cooking, others bake, some combine fresh, raw vegetables to make delicious salads and side dishes, and others smoke-cure meats, freeze-dry fruits and vegetables, or mix herbs and spices for sauces, teas and condiments. These people use the same raw ingredients available to everyone and create foods and beverages that are often unique and better than any similar products available on the market. Calling such culinary wizards "cooks" doesn't seem quite accurate, and the term "foodcrafting" was chosen instead because it is broader and alludes to the creative talent involved.

For those interested in pursuing it, foodcrafting offers numerous advantages. Most importantly, foodcrafting allows you to turn a passion for food into financial rewards. It offers the satisfaction of doing what you love and being your own boss. In some foodcrafting businesses, you have the freedom to choose your own hours by accepting and refusing work as you want. You can start with a minimal time investment and work your way into full-time self-employment at your own pace. If you have another job, foodcrafting can be a good supplementary income, and you can keep your present job until your foodcrafting income justifies quitting.

Most foodcrafting businesses can be started with a low investment if you know how to budget your money. This book will give you tips on doing that, and can save you a bundle if you follow its suggestions. In many cases, you can start your foodcrafting business in your own kitchen, although zoning and health codes make this difficult or even illegal in some locations, so be sure to check.

Another advantage of foodcrafting is the high markups that are often possible. Gross profit margins of 30 to 40 percent are typical for many gourmet foods, compared with an average 7 to 12 percent profit for non-gourmet foods. Although there are no guarantees of becoming rich in foodcrafting, the potential is definitely there. You can see that again and again in the examples given throughout this book of creative foodcrafters who have built thriving businesses from a simple idea. Starting with nothing more than a few business basics and a willingness to work hard, some foodcrafters have built multimillion dollar businesses. Others have succeeded on a smaller scale, but reap the same rewards in satisfaction and fulfillment. The examples are all the more inspiring because they can be repeated by others, including you.

Foodcrafting businesses also offer certain tax advantages. If you work from your home you may be able to deduct a portion of your mortgage payments and your utilities as business expenses.

Restaurant meals can be deductible as research expenses, and purchases of cookware, food, equipment, hired help, advertising, cookbooks, and cooking classes may also be deductible. Be sure to check with your accountant to be sure about each possible deduction.

Many foodcrafting businesses can be used as a springboard to thrust you into other, related businesses. Takeout stores often expand into mail-order businesses or food wholesaling; caterers may open their own take-out shop featuring the foods most requested by satisfied customers; cooking teachers lead gastronomic tours, write cookbooks and become media chefs, and on and on it goes.

Finally, foodcrafting is fun. It allows plenty of room for creative expression, and many of those interviewed for this book stressed the importance of being able to use their kitchen talent to create special foods for other people. They enjoy working with their hands, and they especially appreciate the smile on the face of a satisfied customer.

If you enjoy working creatively with food, this book will guide you through the steps you need to take in starting your own foodcrafting business. We'll give you examples of people who have succeeded in a variety of foodcrafting ventures, tell you what characteristics they discovered are important to success, discuss *why* they succeeded and the lessons they learned about unexpected pitfalls and problems. Then we'll give you tips on financing your business and keeping it in the black.

If you enjoy cooking, have a good head for business, and you're willing to work hard for a few years to get your foodcrafting business off the ground, you're a good candidate for success in this dynamic, growing field.

Chapter 2
Specialty Foodcrafting

Have you ever wondered if you could make money by packaging and selling your rich, creamy fudge? A great idea, you may have thought, but can anyone compete with Nestle and General Mills? Yes, they can! A close look at the package labels in your local supermarket, convenience store, or gourmet food shop may turn up some surprises for you. The food manufacturing business, once almost monopolized by giant food processing companies, is undergoing radical changes. Although the giants of food processing are still very much in evidence on grocery store shelves, specialty foods—often locally produced and much fresher than the nationally available name brand foods—are increasingly evident.

The market for specialty foods is rapidly growing. An enormous shift in family structures and eating habits has caused families to move away from home-cooked, meat-and-potatoes meals in favor of the uniqueness and convenience of specialty foods. During a time when just about everyone is worried about rising prices, unemployment, and hard economic times, imaginative entrepreneurs are proving that America is still the land of opportunity for those with a dream, a little faith, and the will to work for success.

One of those entrepreneurs is John Patton, owner of a fresh fruit and vegetable juice company in Boulder, Colorado. John's involvement in specialty foodcrafting began when Andrea, his wife, discovered she suffered from hypoglycemia, a low blood sugar condition which causes sudden fatigue and, in the worse cases, physical collapse.

"She had a collapse one day, and it startled me," John recalled. "So I started looking into it, and it turned out that the only way they had of treating it was through nutrition. . . . So we went on a crash nutritional program, and within a year she was totally cured of it. . . . I thought (it) was just amazing that you could do that with food."

The new diet not only solved Andrea's blood sugar problem, it also infused the Pattons with so much energy that a return to old eating habits became unthinkable. More and more, their diet included unprocessed foods, raw vegetables, and fresh fruit and vegetable juices. A marvelous source of nutrients and a boon for the digestive system, fresh juices became a staple for the Pattons, but their limited availability on the local market forced John to become an expert in concocting his own: fresh, pulpy apple juice, pure carrot juice, and a "green juice" that included celery, two kinds of lettuce, spinach, and other green vegetables.

After moving to Boulder, John began thinking about starting a business of his own. A former biology student with no background in business, he wasn't sure what he wanted to do, but he kept thinking about his juice creations. "And I thought, 'Well, what better business to do than what I really believe in,' so I thought I wanted to go into manufacturing juice." When he heard of a small juice company willing to sell out, it was a "dream come true." "It was a real small company," he recalls, "but it was up and running, and it was exactly what I wanted."

With $2,000 down, John bought the business and moved into the plant. The first year was tough. John took out very little money for personal use, plowing the rest of the profits back into the business and learning everything he could about purchasing, marketing, distribution, packaging, labeling, and accounting. But a strong commitment to educating people about the benefits of healthy foods and a desire to provide at least a part of that good nutrition himself kept him going, and the work paid off.

In 1982 John distributed his juices, along with other natural foods from area producers, to 54 retail outlets, and his business grossed $240,000. With a contract pending for distribution to Safeway stores and an eye on producing freeze-dried juice, John is gearing up for a national market and hopes to see his juices become a common sight on American dining tables. With an excellent product line and a commitment to "make this my life," John's potential for continued success appears certain.

John's story, although inspiring, isn't really all that unusual. In fact, there are many, many specialty food products now on the market which were once no more than an idea in the mind of a single person.

There are no clear-cut formulas to tell you which specialty foods will become thriving successes, but by knowing your market, researching all costs of production, making your product truly distinctive and standing behind it with a total commitment, you'll enormously improve your chances of success.

STARTING ON A SHOESTRING

With $2,000 down, John Patton bought a tiny juice manufacturing company and, within five years, turned it into a successful business grossing $240,000 a year. Gloria Gilbert bought a few hundred dollars' worth of supplies, started cooking rice pudding from her home kitchen, and, two years later, Fresh! Foods had sales of $37,000. With $1,500 borrowed against his car and family furniture, John Holzmeister started a cheesecake business worth $4 million in 1980. (By 1983 he wouldn't quote his annual gross revenues.)

The beauty of specialty foodcrafting is that it can often be started so cheaply. Many companies which initially invested only enough to cover the cost of ingredients and packaging supplies are now thriving, as the examples above illustrate. Your investment needs will largely depend on the nature of your product, the kitchen that you use, the laws covering food manufacturing in your area, and your own ingenuity. This chapter will give you tips on finding a kitchen to fit your financial and production needs, finding inexpensive equipment and cookware, saving on remodeling costs, and coping with the laws covering food businesses. The ingenuity we'll leave to you!

In 1975 Wally ("Famous") Amos added a few more nuts and chocolate chips to a cookie recipe created in 1929 by Ruth Wakefield, and turned a dream into a business worth $5 million by 1981. John Holzmeister, a former railcar chef with a degree in food service management, dabbled with his wife's cheesecake recipe and, in 1980, reported gross revenues of $4 million. But for every success story there are several failures, and what works in one location may fall flat in another. Before you gamble your job and your lifetime savings on your grandmother's fudge recipe, learn everything you can about the market where you plan to sell your product, and ask yourself these questions:

• *Is it unique?* If your product is similar to a dozen others on the market, develop at least one feature that will make it distinct from them. That may be a lower price, the absence of additives or preservatives, or your absolute insistence on using the finest ingredients available. With lots of cheesecakes already on the market, John Holzmeister found his niche by using only the best cream cheese he could find and by refusing to whip in air bubbles. This dedication to quality brought him a dozen orders in his first two hours of business.

• *Can you produce the product without pricing yourself out of the market?* If your chocolate chip cake draws rave reviews from everyone you know but costs an arm and a leg to make, you may not be able to sell to a large enough market to make a profit. Be sure to check area supermarkets, health food stores and gourmet food shops for similar items, noting their price and ingredients. Because they buy in such large quantities, big manufacturers can generally afford to price their products lower than small companies.

• *What is the shelf life of your product? Will it survive shipping, packaging, and idle time on the shelf of your distributor?* This is of critical importance if you expect to produce fresh foods or beverages, and will dramatically limit your available market. If the shelf life is extremely short, plan on marketing only in your local area.

• *What is your level of commitment to your business?* This may be the most important factor in determining business success. As John Patton said, "I would never advise anybody to do anything on a small business basis unless they really believed in the product, and I would advise them not to do it just for the money. They have to really believe in it, because it takes so much effort." For John, like most small wholesalers, that commitment meant working long hours the first year, working to develop a line of products which meant more than a paycheck to him. "There've been many times when I've sat at my desk with my head in my hands going, 'Why am I doing this to myself?" he said. "Then the next day I'd see some kid drinking the juice, and I'd think 'That's why I'm doing it.' The level of commitment is crucial."

• *Is your target market large enough?* While fried rice sandwiches may sell well in a health-conscious town like Boulder, Colorado, it's doubtful that they would bring a profit in most rural communities. One of the biggest reasons that certain products fail in one market while being a hit in another is that the manufacturer didn't know the market.

• *Can you expand your original idea into other foods?* John Holzmeister thinks he was lucky to begin selling quality cheesecake at a time when just about everyone seemed to want it. But recently he's begun thinking about new product lines because, he says, "It won't be long before people are eating something else, and they won't buy cheesecake anymore.'' He also feels that there are so many competitors in the quality cheesecake business now that his market is being squeezed.

Steve Bernstein greatly expanded the market for his Grateful Sandwiches when he introduced pre-packaged bagels with cream cheese. A hit for many years on the east coast, it was almost unknown in Denver, Grateful Sandwiches' home base. Today, a single account sells 500 bagels a week, and the market continues to grow.

You can take a tip from McDonald's when you think about building an empire based on a single product: It may work fine to initally catch the attention of consumers, but sooner or later they'll be asking for variations and completely new products.

What It Takes to Succeed

Gloria Gilbert made her first food sale to a health food market in 1980. It was for five pounds of amasake, a Japanese rice pudding, "and I was a nervous wreck," Gloria laughingly recalls. Taking a friend along "for moral support," she drummed up enough courage to approach the store manager and ask for a trial run with the pudding. Despite Gloria's shaking knees, the manager agreed, and told her to call back in a few days. "I was so nervous and so sure it wouldn't sell, I didn't call back for ten days!" she recalls. But the amasake sold out quickly, and a whole new lifestyle for Gloria was ushered in with the first reorder.

A cocktail waitress for nine years before beginning her foodcrafting venture, Gloria was used to long nights, late mornings and unpredictable schedules. The switch from employee to business owner was a drastic one, she said. "When you're into the bar lifestyle there isn't much responsibility. You can always get somebody to cover your shift, and everyone's drunk, so it doesn't matter if you are, too. Owning my own business and working with food that I strongly believe in . . . made me much more responsible.''

Today, Gloria is the successful owner and president of Fresh! Foods, a macrobiotic food wholesaling company that produces a line of grain- and vegetable-based salads, sandwiches, burgers and desserts. Fresh! Foods grossed about $37,000 in 1982—not a fortune, but adequate for Gloria's present needs. With accounts pending through a state-wide supermarket chain and a chain of convenience stores, the potential for expansion looks good to Gloria, who is a little surprised at her rapid growth.

"When I started the business," she said, "it was kind of a side hobby. I didn't really expect it to get big, and I didn't really expect to be a businesswoman." Her primary concern in the beginning was to produce a line of wholesome, fresh foods, rather than to make a lot of money. Taking out less than $800 a month for living expenses, she put the remaining profits back into the business, a practice she continues today.

Like most successful business owners, Gloria's commitment is total. During her company's first year, she often began work in her pajamas and cooked from the wee hours of morning until late afternoon. "I couldn't just call in sick and take the day off to go skiing," she said. "I had to be there myself to cover all aspects of the business." She made do with her own rough purchasing, distributing and accounting systems, and worked out of her home to save money. For months at a time, she was "absolutely broke," but the business never suffered and, after nine months, she had saved enough to move the operation into a rented kitchen. There she learned her first hard lesson about the business world.

"A man that I was working with stole one of my recipes and started making the same sandwich!" she recalls, still with disbelief. "I was just so, so upset. I was like a little girl; I didn't know what to do, and I just cried and cried." Then, when her anger began to surface, she called all of the man's accounts, told them of the incident, and moved out of the building. But it had taught her an indispensable lesson: "I had to learn a business sense, that it wasn't all personal. Now, there's a business side to my life and there's a personal side to my life, and the two don't mix."

Asked what kept her going during the tough early days, she replied, "I guess my belief in what I'm doing. "I've never worked as hard in my life, and there were times I didn't want to do it anymore. . . . But that's it: belief in the integrity of the product and seeing what owning my own business is doing for me."

For Gloria, like many other business owners, building a successful business has more to do with commitment to an idea than with following strict principles of business management. But part of that commitment involves a willingness to learn, and the more you know about marketing, distributing and accounting, the better off you'll be.

A lot of foodcrafters have made a good living without any business background at all. John Patton was a biologist just out of school when he bought Rainbow Juices, and a complete lack of business training only meant that he had to work a little harder to be a success. "I learned by doing," he said. "I asked questions of my friends, read whatever books, magazines and articles I could pick up, listened whenever I could." When faced with a decision on designing new labels, a subject John knew absolutely nothing about and couldn't afford to pay someone to teach him, he thumbed through the Yellow Pages and called all the packaging companies listed, asking "Do you have a few minutes? We don't know anything about this, and we need some education. Do you have any brochures you can send us?" Before long, John knew everything he needed to know about labeling, and had made some new friends, too.

"People are very, very helpful," he said. "I've had men who were very high in very large companies get on the phone and just talk . . . as long as I wanted to talk to them, and give me quite a bit of information."

The rewards of owning one's own business go far beyond the profits to be made, and if you're willing to work hard for the first few years, asking questions, weathering setbacks and looking ahead to the future, you've got what it takes to become successful.

The Importance of Studying Your Market

One of the best ways to ensure the success of your new business is to thoroughly understand the market you're serving.

That doesn't mean you should pay thousands of dollars to have a professional market research firm conduct an in-depth study, complete with charts, graphs, and reams of statistics. You can produce most of the information you need by conducting your own informal study.

In order to determine the image that will best sell your product, it's important to understand the personality of your target market. The market for fudge brownies may be entirely different from the market for herbed vinegars, and by determining what your target market is like you'll begin to understand how to approach it most effectively.

U.S. Census Bureau statistics are one of the best sources of demographic information. By studying them, you can learn the median age, income level, and buying and eating habits in your particular area. Armed with this information, you should visit area restaurants, supermarkets, specialty shops, and other food outlets, noting the types of patrons served by each. Who are they? What do they buy? Are they likely to buy your product there, or would they go somewhere else to look for it? What is their income level? Are they willing to pay extra for gourmet specialty foods, or are they more interested in hunting for bargains? Do they carefully read labels, or is it fancy packaging that seems to appeal to them most?

Be sure, too, that you understand the personality of the restaurants or stores where you plan to sell your products. What types of foods are sold there? How would your product fit in? How are various foods grouped together? What is the most desirable display area or menu classification for your product?

Referring to sales to restaurants, John Holzmeister points out that "The big secret . . . is to make something that's already on the menu. I've seen companies come and go by the score which had good products, but no one wanted to print up new menus to get them." If your product is completely new and you're determined to market to restaurants and institutions, try having cards printed that describe your product and can be easily inserted inside of menus or displayed on counters.

After you've selected the best market for your product, it's time to test it out. Try it on your friends, serve it at dinner parties.

Enter food fairs, bazaars, bake sales. And everywhere, ask questions: How do you like this carrot cake? Would you buy it in a store? How much would you pay for it? Do you shop once a month? Twice? How often would you be likely to buy it? How many people are in your family? Would they like it too? How much money do you spend a month on snacks and gourmet items? You may wish to pass out a questionnaire with each sale—many people will be happy to answer your questions, and you may get some valuable tips on how to market your product to its fullest potential.

Doing a market study may take a little time, but the results can be well worth it. Many companies initially began without any marketing information other than their own "gut feelings," and a fair number of them have been successful. But knowing your market, its size, its characteristics and its ability to pay for your product will be one of your best hedges against failure. And, store and restaurant managers are as impressed as anyone else by professionalism. Your ability to describe the personality of their customers, explain how your product would fit in, and tell why his customers would buy it will go a long way in winning over your first account.

EARLY DECISIONS

What's in a Name?

You may not have thought about it much, but the name you choose for your company can become one of your best marketing tools. Gloria Gilbert instantly transformed a simple name into a real attention-grabber with the use of punctuation: Fresh! Foods was chosen to conjure up images of crisp and wholesome goodness. Those familiar with Greek literature will recognize Dionysos Heavenly Foods as truly devine. A Greek mythological character, Dionysos is known as the god of food, wine, and sensual pleasure. And who could resist the temptation of Audrey's No-No's, a sinfully delicious line of pastries and candies made even more appealing because they are forbidden. Your company name is important. It deserves plenty of thought and all of your imagination.

Wholesale or Retail?

There are basically two ways to sell your products: wholesale or retail. To decide which is best for you, ask yourself these questions, and honestly consider your answers. Of course, it may be that you'll be successful at both!

• Are you good with people? Are you a charmer who can sell just about anything with your smile? Or are you happier in the kitchen than in a crowd? If you love to be where the action is, you'll love retailing. As a wholesaler, you'll deal primarily with people in other businesses, making sales calls and depending on them to sell your products for you.

• Can you produce you foods, package them, do the books, purchase supplies, and still have time to set up retail distribution? Can you hire someone else to do it for you, without sacrificing too much control? Or is your time better spent encouraging others to market your products from their store or restaurant?

• Can you afford to wholesale and still make a good living? Because you make a much higher profit per item when you eliminate the retailer and go directly to the consumer, you should carefully consider how much each market would satisfy your financial needs.

There are advantages and disadvantages to both wholesaling and retailing, of course. You should consider all factors before deciding against one in favor of the other. Although your oven-fresh chocolate chip cookies may bring a 300 to 400 percent profit when you sell directly to the consumer, wholesaling operations typically have a much broader market penetration. Even if you hire enough teenagers to sell your cookies in every park and mall in town, they still can't match the exposure that dozens of retail outlets and restaurants could bring.

Before you decide on just one type of marketing approach, remember that you can double your money by doubling your exposure. A customer who enjoys your cheesecake in his favorite restaurant will probably be delighted to find it in his local grocery store. And he might appreciate the opportunity to buy it at its freshest by going directly to the source.

Once you've decided whether to wholesale or retail your products, there are other options to consider. If you plan to wholesale your products, will they do better in a convenience store, restaurant, supermarket, or health food store? Delis, vending trucks, pushcarts, sundry shops, office and institutional cafeterias, resorts and recreational areas all offer sales possibilities.

Do you plan to retail your products without a middleman? Again, your success potential will directly match your ingenuity. With a portable table draped with cloth and a friendly smile you can set up a booth in flea markets, bazaars, a busy park, or anywhere there is heavy pedestrian traffic (providing there are no restrictions against soliciting). Farmers have sold fresh fruits and vegetables, canned goods, and homemade meat products from the back of trucks on rural highways for generations. What's to stop you from doing the same? Have you ever considered selling your specialty at a high school or college sports event? At a concert? On the beach? If you have trouble picturing yourself as a peddler, hire some youngsters to do it for you on a commission basis. They'll appreciate the job, and you'll make a good day's profit and gain exposure. Be sure, though, to explore the laws and restrictions covering your type of vending. Concert halls, football stadiums, beaches and other popular gathering places may have contracts with one exclusive vendor which would prohibit the sale of your products. Solicitation may even be outlawed altogether. Still, there are usually plenty of places which will let you sell your goods (sometimes for a share of the profits) and you'll do well to try them all at least once.

Your Retail Marketing Skills

Have you ever noticed the difference in vendors at fairs and bazaars? While one sits, somber and bored, with only an occasional customer venturing near, another is surrounded by a growing, happy crowd of customers. This vendor thrives on human contact and thrills his customers with a constant stream of patter and antics. With a ready smile and a friendly manner, he manages to keep track of a dozen things at once: he can take your order, pop the food in a bag, ring up the sale, give you your change, make a wisecrack about your daughter's pigtails and brightly turn to the next customer before you know the sale has been made! By the end of the day this vendor's been well paid for his performance with a cash register that's three times as full as anyone else's.

You don't have to be an actor or actress to be a good retailer, but it helps to have a little chutzpah and a genuine love for the public. You want to cultivate a knowledge of your customers, and recognize people by name if they stop by often. Pay attention to the suggestions and advice they give you; listen to their comments as they talk about your product. Never assume that your product is so perfect it can't be improved. By realizing that your customers are valuable and important, you'll not only gain new insights into your business but make a lot of friends, too.

One of the best ways to advertise your business is to get someone else to do it for you. Satisfied customers will do a good job of word-of-mouth advertising, but you can increase your chances of becoming an overnight success by seeking out free publicity. Send (or, better yet, personally deliver) your product to newspaper food editors, television and radio food show hosts, and anyone else who can provide media exposure for your product. One good write-up can deluge you with requests and triple your sales, so be sure you're ready for it when it happens.

Your Wholesale Marketing Skills

Whether you're selling to a fancy restaurant or the corner deli, your prospective wholesale buyer will want to know he's dealing with a professional. He's probably seen plenty of small food producers come and go, and before you open your mouth he'll be sizing you up with silent observations. A neat appearance and confident attitude will help get you in the door, but you'll need to follow it up with the kind of information that he's looking for:

• *Know his business!* Nothing flatters a business owner as much as someone understanding and genuinely appreciating the hard work they have put into making their business successful. If you can intelligently discuss the businessman's operation and his customers, you'll be a step closer to getting your order.

• *Know how your product fits his store or restaurant image.* Does his menu or product line currently include your competitor's products? If so, you must convince him of the superiority of your products over those he already buys. If not, you must convince him to expand his line to include them. Your knowledge of the way products are grouped in the store will help you to suggest appropriate areas for each item you produce. Any brochures or small displays you can supply which match the image of his store or restaurant may give you a better shot at desirable eye-level shelf space.

• *Bring a sample of your product.* Nothing convinces like taste, especially if you're up against established competition. If you use quality, top-of-the-line ingredients, be sure to emphasize it. Assure your buyer that your quality level will be consistent. Natural food outlets will want to know about your use of chemicals and preservatives. You should assure them that you'll let them know of any changes you make in the ingredients you use.

• *Provide pricing information.* Because you're a new company, your prospective customers may be leery of frequent price increases. Assure each buyer that your price structure allows a margin for inflation and will remain unchanged

for at least a year, if at all possible. Because you're capitaliz-
ing a new business, your prices will probably have to be a little
higher than normal to cover the cost of your initial investment, overhead and equipment. Convince the buyer that your
commitment to quality justifies your price and offer a trial
run to let your customer decide whether it's worth the price he
has to charge to get his own percentage. More often than not,
he'll discover that customers are willing to pay a little more
for quality and he will soon have a reorder for you.

• *Provide payment terms and delivery dates.* How often
will you deliver your products? Is there a minimum order requirement? The shelf life of your product and the needs of the
buyer will determine whether you must deliver three times a
week or only once. What about payment terms? Most restaurants and retail outlets are on 30 to 60 day terms with other
suppliers, and to stay in the business you'll probably have to
match that. Some managers will understand your predica-
ment as a new company, however, and may be willing to pay
you at the time of delivery. Either way, be sure to provide an
invoice and payment receipt. You can buy pre-printed forms
and stamp them with your company name and address to save
the cost of custom printing.

• *Provide storage and cooking information.* What kind
of storage space does your product require? Does it need to be
refrigerated? Can it be taken directly from the freezer and put
in an oven or microwave? What are the cooking requirements? Can it be refrozen after cooking or thawing? What is
the shelf life? The easier it is to store and handle your product, the easier your product will sell, so emphasize simplicity
when providing information on handling requirements.

Not all of your customers will need all of the above information, but you'll increase your confidence and persuasive skills if
you arrive well-prepared for your first sales call. Part of the secret
of making a sale, according to Su-Lin Mosier, part-owner of

Please do not turn down
the corners of the pages
Use a book mark.

Dionysos Heavenly Foods, is being able to size up a potential buyer within the first few minutes. "Some people you go in and sell," she said, "and with some people you go in and start a conversation." Of course there are a few people who won't even talk to you, a fact that can be devastating if you're selling for the first time and a little timid about talking to business owners, as Steve Bernstein of Grateful Sandwiches found out.

"I used to go out (on sales calls)" he said. "I was terrible! I took it all too personally, I guess." For the Bernsteins, the problem was a brand new product with little competition (and therefore little familiarity) on the market. "It was kind of a new thing here in Denver—wholesaling vegetarian sandwiches," Steve remembered. "So a lot of people wouldn't even give you a shot." Grateful sandwiches were turned down by supermarkets, convenience stores, hospitals, office buildings and health food stores that first year, and "it was real discouraging at first," Steve lamented. Now Steve doesn't have to make sales calls. "For the most part people just call us. . . . (They) will be waiting when the driver arrives!" Steve said, exultant over the current popularity of his sandwiches. Even some of those who initially refused to handle the sandwiches have come around, and "people who wouldn't even let us take the product out of the box have called me and have ended up being good accounts years later." But the turnaround didn't happen overnight, and Steve learned at an early date to supplement his wholesale business by entering food fairs and street bazaars on weekends, a great idea for increasing exposure and introducing people to a new line of food.

If you're absolutely terrible at making sales calls, or if you find the production part of your business taking up all of your time, you can hire others to do your selling for you. Most salespeople work on a commission basis, usually under 10 percent of the total sale. In addition, food brokers will represent your product to accounts they regularly visit for a flat fee or a commission. You can find them listed under Food Brokerage Firms in the Yellow Pages. If you sell to a number of restaurants, you may want to talk with the restaurant supply houses that regularly call on your restaurant accounts. Supply houses will generally charge a commission on the sales they make for you, and they may also want a monthly or annual fee for representing your product. The cost of hiring a salesman or brokerage firm could cut so deeply into your profits that it wouldn't be worthwhile, so carefully consider all costs before signing any agreements.

Keeping on top of the market is an important requirement for success in the specialty foodcrafting business. By leaving most experimentation up to smaller companies, traditional food manufacturers have forfeited a profitable share of the market. That's good for you, but be sure not to make the same mistake by becoming stagnate yourself. Go to food fairs and check out new trends in foods, packaging, labeling and storage. Talk to other foodcrafters and keep abreast of national and local news. Experiment with variations of your product and complementary items. You can never know too much so keep asking questions and keep your mind open for new ideas. According to John Patton, the potential success of your business is directly related to your ability to understand what your market is, what your customers want now, and how to keep them satisfied in the future. "It's all marketing skills," he says. "Of course, once they try it, if it's not any good, they're not going to buy it a second time."

Finding a Kitchen

There is nothing new about people making money from their kitchens. For years people have baked cakes and cookies to be sold at church or community bazaars, bolstered family incomes with scrumptious divinity or deep dish apple pies, and canned sweet maple syrup and home-grown bing cherries to be sold in local markets. With the right combination of quality ingredients and the will to turn your foodcrafting into a business, you too can make money from your kitchen.

Cooking for profit from the home is as viable today as it ever has been—probably more so. Gloria Gilbert's home was her office for nine months before Fresh! Foods outgrew her counter space and home oven. Joanna Walpole moved her salad making business back into her home kitchen after she awoke one morning and decided she didn't want to go to work. Farmers still make sausage, cheeses, canned fruits and pickles to be sold at farmer's markets, and it sometimes seems that every family in Vermont with a maple tree has canned syrup and sold it to vacationers passing by.

Because of the highly perishable nature of some foods, however, producing food products for sale out of home kitchens is illegal in many communities, and health departments are becoming increasingly strict in dealing with those found operating without the proper licenses. To find out whether you can use your kitchen for a foodcrafting operation, check with local zoning and health officials. Although "bootleg" operations sometimes survive outside of the law for years at a time, it's really not worth taking the risk.

If you can't cook from your kitchen, there are numerous other options that can save you the expense and frustration of remodeling a rented space to bring it up to compliance with health department regulations. Among the possibilities for renting a previously approved kitchen are other food manufacturers, summer camps, resorts, university cafeterias, company cafeterias, restaurants, churches, civic and community halls, and cooking schools.

In fact, any organization which uses an approved kitchen for limited periods may welcome the opportunity for rental income when their kitchen is not in use. Before you sign a lease, though, be sure the hours available for your use of the kitchen are fully acceptable to you. Cooking from midnight until 8 a.m. may get you a lower rent, but can create havoc with your family life. You also want to be certain the the kitchen fully complies with local health and zoning regulations for your particular operation. A kitchen set up for sandwich making probably won't do if you have to use fryers or meat processors in your operation. If you have trouble locating an adequate kitchen, your health department may be able to help. With their thorough knowledge of approved area kitchens, they may be able to point out the perfect facility for your business.

It is not uncommon for several foodcrafting businesses to share a common production facility. By doing so, they can drastically reduce rent costs and equipment purchases. Schedules can be arranged according to the time and space requirements of each company. While John Patton makes his fresh juices in one part of the Rainbow Juice plant, for example, Gloria Gilbert uses another section half time to produce her rice pudding. Two other companies arrange to use the facility one or two hours a week as needed.

Among the advantages of sharing kitchen space with other foodcrafters is the exchange of ideas and techniques and the warm comraderie that develops among people working toward common goals. When Gloria Gilbert dropped out of the bar and cocktailing world, she found an entirely different type of people among fellow foodcrafters. "Now all of my friends are in this business," she says. They compare notes on new product ideas, marketing strategies, pricing methods and general food trends.

If you're lucky, you'll find someone like John Patton to help you along in your new business. John clearly remembers the hardships of his early days just starting out, and he's willing to share his hard-won business knowledge with just about anyone who asks. Through him, Gloria Gilbert and many other young foodcrafters have learned about pricing, bookkeeping, marketing, inventory, purchasing and distribution. Referring to his generosity in helping others, John said "I think it's the responsibility of those businesses that have made it to help. . . . Everybody has to have help from somebody else; otherwise they can't make it."

If You Must Remodel

If you can't find an adequate kitchen to rent, you may be forced to consider remodeling an existing building to fit your needs. Remodeling can be tremendously expensive, though, and health department rules are usually more strict when you start from scratch rather than taking over an established kitchen. To comply with Denver health department rules, the Bernsteins spent over $13,000 getting their production facility up to par, which included putting in new floor tiles, replacing acoustical ceiling tiles with drywall, sanding down "grainy" walls and repainting them to the health department's specifications. Then they needed a three-compartment sink for washing dishes and rinsing food, and a separate sink for washing their hands. By the time their building passed inspection, they barely had enough money left to produce their first batch of sandwiches.

The most important point to remember as you remodel your kitchen space is to check with all governmental authorities who may have a say in how you do the work. While the fire department may not care if you install indoor/outdoor carpeting in your kitchen, the health department will probably demand tile or another easy-to-clean surface. A trial and error approach to remodeling could prove disasterous.

If you're handy with a hammer, you may be able to save yourself a bundle of money by doing much of the work yourself. You can hire an independent contractor for the more difficult parts of the job and check with him on all of the work you do—but don't be talked into letting him do it all if you can do much of it just as easily yourself. In finding a contractor you can trust, talk to the Better Business Bureau and building supply stores for recommendations, and call people for whom the contractor has recently worked. The extra time you spend in finding out about your contractor's workmanship could save you untold headaches down the road.

THE NUTS AND BOLTS

Equipment

Rounding up the right equipment for your foodcrafting business can be exasperating and expensive, but by researching the equipment market as well as you research the market for your products, you can probably cut your expenses in half. To begin with, try to rent a kitchen that already has most of the equipment you need. At the Rainbow Juice plant, four companies share refrigerators, freezers, ovens, mixers and storage space. Most institutional kitchens, community and civic lodges, resorts and restaurants will include equipment use in the rent they charge you, and you may be able to split the cost of new equipment you buy with them. Getting to know the manager of the space you rent could pay off when you look for equipment—not only can he give you the names of suppliers who deal in second-hand equipment, but he'll probably know the best servicemen. Larger restaurants and institutions often get special prices on equipment, and they may allow you to use their account, or set up a sub-account in their name, so you can benefit from the same price reductions. At the least, a good word from the manager of your kitchen may get special attention for you.

Most equipment companies have rental/purchase plans or leasing options for larger pieces of equipment. Because they own the equipment, the leasing company will usually make repairs on the equipment at no cost, and lease payments are tax deductible. Leasing contracts usually run for one to five years. At the end of that time, you have the option to purchase the equipment or continue leasing, often with new equipment. There are other advantages to leasing, but remember: with interest on each payment, you'll be paying a premium price for the equipment in the long run. Check and compare terms with many different companies to get the price and the purchase options that are best for you.

Bankruptcy sales, auctions and surplus liquidations can be excellent sources of good equipment and even vehicles. John Patton bought his first delivery van, in exceptional condition, for $550 from a telephone company surplus sale and advises that utility companies sell their trucks and vans at equally low prices. Army surplus auctions are notorious for good buys, and they often include everything from jeeps to huge kitchen kettles, mixers, and appliances. If your newspaper doesn't provide information on sales of this kind, contact the appropriate utility company or armed service for information. Your bank may also know of pending bankruptcies and may be able to give you some good inside tips on when liquidation proceedings will begin. Because these sales are often packed with bargain hunters, you may wish to get a list of the items to be sold from the auctioneer or sale official to study before the sale begins. Get there early, and check out the equipment closely. Remember that regardless of how cheaply you make a purchase, it's not a good buy if you have to spend a fortune on repairs.

When purchasing new or used equipment from a dealer,

always compare prices, brand names, age and the condition of the equipment, and name the prices you've been quoted by other dealers. That may not make you popular with the dealers, but it will assure you the lowest price and fairest deal.

If the company you buy from doesn't make service calls, it's a good idea to line up a few reputable service contractors who can be called any time of the day or night. An oven breakdown at six o'clock Friday evening will cost you a lot more than repairs if you can't get it fixed until nine o'clock Monday morning. Don't pick just any company in the Yellow Pages. Like auto mechanics, some equipment repairmen do better work and are more reliable than others. If they're good, they won't hesitate to give you the names of other customers they service. Call them! Spend a few minutes with them, asking questions like, "How quickly does the company respond to service calls?" "How often do you need repairs on your equipment?" "Does the repair work hold up, or do you often find yourself calling again in a few weeks?" "Are their prices fair?" Most people will be glad to spend the few minutes you ask for, and the information you gain from such calls can be invaluable when you are forced to really depend on your service company.

Legalities

Many, many foodcrafting businesses have begun in family kitchens, and some are legally allowed to continue as cottage industries. Others have been forced to find a rental kitchen in a hurry or to shut down completely when irate health officials discovered that their home food business was operating illegally. To avoid any chance of this happening to you, learn everything you can about the laws covering your business in your locality. Not only will this save you frustration in the long run, it will probably save you money. Trying to find a kitchen that fits all of your needs on a week's notice can cause you to lose both business and sleep.

Among the licenses and permits you may have to secure in opening up your foodcrafting business are the following:

     • *License To Operate a Food Service Establishment*, or the

equivalent, from your county or city health department. It will usually require a complete floor plan of the building you intend to use, and a detailed description of the equipment you'll have and how you plan to use it. In addition, you'll need to prove you have proper product liability coverage, as well as fire and theft insurance in some localities.

• *Federal, state, county or city tax identification numbers*, where applicable. While wholesalers do not charge sales taxes in some areas, many communities nevertheless require a tax i.d. number and monthly tax reports.

• *Zoning Permit*

• *Fire Inspection Certificate*

• *Proof of Unemployment Compensation payments*

• *Proof of Workman's Compensation Insurance payments*

All of this can be confusing, if not expensive. Talk to other food manufacturers in your area for tips on dealing with each authority and keeping it all straight. Then call each branch of government involved with your type of business, and call and call again. Government officials are notorious for not knowing what other authorities will require or which step should be taken first, and running through the red tape can be maddening. Be sure to know all the steps required before making any move to rent or buy your kitchen space.

Pricing

What price is a good price? That depends on the nature of your product, your overhead expenses, and who buys your product. Though it costs more to make, a macrobiotic salad will bring a much lower profit than, say, a giant chocolate chip cookie. Steve Bernstein, owner of Grateful Sandwiches, told us "You always hear that . . . in the food business, charge four times your material costs. You can't do that with natural foods, or you'll price yourself out of the market." That's because the cost of "natural" ingredients is often two to three times higher than processed ingredients, he said. To compensate, Steve charges only about 35 to 40 percent over his cost of producing the products.

The formula that John Patton uses for determining retail prices can be helpful. It is called the "F.L.O." system of pricing because it involves adding annual food, labor and overhead expenses to arrive at an annual production expense. After determining the number of units he plans to produce, John divides that into the sum of the F.L.O. Next he subtracts the amount of profit he wants to realize from 100 percent, and divides the diference into the sum of the F.L.O. per unit. If he planned to produce 100,000 gallons of juice and his operating costs are $100,000, for example, he must charge $1.66 a gallon to make a 40 percent profit. It might look like this on his books:

Annual Production Expense

Food Cost............$23,000
Labor Cost............27,000
Overhead..............50,000
Total................$100,000

$100,000 ÷ 100,000 gal. = $1.00

100%
− 40% Profit Expected
60%

$1.00 ÷ .60 = $1.66 per gallon

Whatever formula you use to determine your pricing, be sure

to plan ahead for price increases and inflation. Frequent price hikes for your product can damage your credibility and frighten away your customers.

In the end, your prices for each product will be determined by what the market will bear. People seem willing to pay more for dessert and snack items, so you may wish to use a higher profit on those to compensate for lower profits on salads and sandwiches. To find out what people are willing to pay, ask your friends and neighbors what they would be willing to pay for your product. Try out different prices yourself in limited tests until you hit on one that results in the most sales without sacrificing the profit you need to survive. If you need more information on how to price your products, pick up the pamphlets the Small Business Administration publishes on the subject or talk with other food producers. More often than not, they'll be willing to share their knowledge and help you along.

Packaging and Labeling

The way you present your product to the public can be just as important as what goes into the package. This is especially true if you plan to market your product in supermarkets and convenience stores. As John Patton says, "The middle class eats with their eyes. In supermarkets they don't read labels . . . they look. They look at the package, they look at the label and what the product looks like inside. And then they'll buy it, based upon those things." Shoppers in health food stores, ethnic markets and the like are a little less picky about what the outer wrapping looks like, it seems. "According to all the shop owners and managers I've talked to," John said, "at least 50 percent of the health food people eat by reading the labels. . . . That's a lot more than in supermarkets."

Because the package and label are the first things a customer sees, they should present the image you want to get across. Image is everything to a new buyer. Are your candies made with old-fashioned care and attention? Antique-looking art on a simple cardboard box will say it for you. Do you can your preserves straight from the farm, or at least want it to look like you do? A swatch of calico or gingham cloth over the top will make the consumer feel like he's sitting right at your country kitchen table. But you don't have to spend half of your budget trying to convey a homespun image: simplicity is always attractive. When a customer picks up one of Gloria Gilbert's hand-wrapped sandwiches, he can almost visualize the care that goes into making, cutting and wrapping each one. What could be more appealing?

Before you decide on any type of packaging, be sure it meets any applicable health code requirements and will both protect your product and fit within your budget requirements. Salads can be placed in simple plastic tubs, sandwiches in pre-shaped, heat-sealed plastic containers, but a cake or delicate pastry will need the protection of corrugated cardboard or molded plastic. If your food is to be frozen, plastic-coated cardboard or plastic containers and wrapping are best. Consider, too, what will be done with the product after it's purchased. Microwave ovens may soon be standard in American kitchens, and you'll have an edge on the competition if your product package can stand the strain of being popped directly from the freezer into the microwave. Remember, also, that the slightest trace of metal in the label or package can short-circuit a microwave oven.

As a small foodcrafter, you'll be able to save money by packaging and labeling your products by hand. But you may find it taking up valuable time as your business expands and need to find a packaging contractor to help you out or else purchase your own equipment.

Packaging contractors are listed in the Yellow Pages under Package Designing and Development, Packaging Materials, and similar headings, and you can learn a lot about the options available simply by calling up several of them. By comparing prices and types of packaging, and by looking at a few of the packages used by each contractor, you'll get a pretty good idea of which is best for you. You may want to call some of the contractors' accounts to find out how quickly they fulfill their orders, the number of defects that can be expected, and their general reliability.

You may be able to buy your own packaging or bottling equipment, and end up saving money in the long run. Your equipment dealer could have used packaging equipment for sale. Check with other food manufacturers too; if you use the same type of packaging, you may be able to split the cost of a machine, or you could buy the equipment yourself and then rent it out to others on a contract basis.

One of the most important parts of your package is the label. (For simplicity, we'll refer to any directions, information, or artwork which appears on a package as its label.) At the very minimum, your label should include a list of ingredients used in your product (listed in order of quantity used), preparation directions, an expiration date, and your company name and address.

The real purpose of your label isn't just to give information, it must also make people want to buy your product. The advertising industry has spent millions of dollars trying to find out what motivates people to buy, and here are a few of their findings:

• *Consumers want value (or at least the appearance of value).* They're not so concerned with the price if, in their minds, it is justified. High quality ingredients, "natural" handling and processing methods, and uniqueness all contribute to price justification.

• *"Gimmicks" can work.* That doesn't mean you should put anything dishonest or unethical on your label or package—a gimmick can be anything from cartoons to coupons and contests. Celestial Seasonings teas create a pleasant, relaxed image for their product with their brightly colored boxes containing directions, information about the tea, and suggestions for its use, all written in a friendly, conversational tone. And to top it all off, each type of tea comes with a different philosophical quotation or aphorism. Consider a sample of the writing from a box of Country Apple Herb Tea:

> About the tea: We call this herb tea Country Apple because its luscious apple flavor unfolds with each sip as the aroma of orchards takes you back to breezy afternoons in the country. With good

old American apples we have combined rosehips
and hibiscus flowers for a bit of tartness,
chamomile and chicory for smoothness and body,
and cinnamon and nutmeg for just the right spice.
Country Apple is an apple adventure.

Doesn't that make you want to try some?

• *Consumers like to think that they're well informed*
about ingredients. But don't just let your customers assume
your company uses only the finest ingredients—tell them! As
John Patton says, "People won't go through the trouble of
reading all the ingredients to find out if your product is made
without sugar. But they'll buy it if you tell them it's made
without sugar! They like to have you spell it out to them."
One way to spell it out is to write it on the front of the
package. Because people are becoming increasingly concerned about good health, you'll do best when you can
honestly prove the natural, wholesome goodness of your
products.

Consumers can be intensely loyal to the companies they trust
and feel close to. Wouldn't you prefer home baked bread from a
friend's foodcrafting venture over nationally marketed brands in
the supermarket? The principle is the same: win the trust and
friendship of a customer, and you can count on repeat business
with him. Although Celestial Seasonings is now a large company
with millions in annual sales revenues, it still retains its homey, intimate image by talking to its customers as friends. In fact, they invite correspondence and suggestions, and often the quotations they
use on their packages are supplied to them by their customers. Who
could possibly switch to another brand of tea after seeing a quotation they supplied on a box of Celestial Seasonings?

Of course, even the best of labels won't help if your customer
loses respect for your company. To promote trust in your company
you should use only the best ingredients and tell only the truth
about your product. If your bread is made with whole grains but

does contain chemical preservatives, you'd better think twice about calling it "natural." Always treat the consumer as you would a member of your family, and you'll win his continued and loyal patronage.

With all of this in mind, you're ready to design and print your labels. If you're good at sketching and composition, at least attempt to design your own.

If you're better at cooking than art, there are plenty of talented people who can help you out. Friends or relatives may love the chance to exercise their talents. John Patton traded 750 gallons of juice for a label one of his employees designed—a bargain for both of them. If you need the help of a professional, you'll find plenty of them listed under Package Designing, Commercial Art, and similar listings in the Yellow Pages. Again, you'll need to check around for prices and quality of work. Different artists have different styles, too, and while one artist may be great with contemporary styles, another may be much better at making your package look like it was designed in the 1800s.

Most package manufacturers can also produce your labels. Be sure to order plenty of them ahead of time, because production time can run as long as a month for large orders. You can cut down on costs by purchasing your own labeling equipment or by sharing with another company. Not only is it less expensive in the long run to produce your own labels, it's also easier to quickly add a new product to your existing product line.

Distributing Your Product

The nature of your product, its shelf life, and the amount you produce will all influence your distribution. A few dozen brownies can be delivered to neighborhood stores and restaurants in the back of a station wagon, but strict health codes will tell you just how cold you must keep dairy products and frozen foods during transportation. When John Patton first bought Rainbow Juices, he produced just enough juice to fit in a few ice boxes in the back of a van. Today, he uses refrigerated trucks to deliver the large quantities of juice he produces each week. John also provides delivery services for other small foodcrafters, which can be a great way to pool resources and save time and energy.

If you sell mainly to restaurant suppliers, you can have them pick up your products and deliver them for you. Otherwise, you can pool with other wholesalers or hire your own driver. To find a good delivery firm, talk to restaurant owners and specialty food store operators, or look under Delivery Services in the Yellow Pages.

With the cost of gasoline and auto repairs on the rise, distribution is becoming more and more expensive. You can usually save money in the long run by buying your own truck or delivery van, and with a little effort, you can find a good deal on an older model at an auction, inventory surplus sale, or bankruptcy liquidation. If you need shelving or refrigeration in the truck, ask your restaurant equipment supplier about used equipment.

MANAGEMENT PERSPECTIVES

Cash Flow and Time Management

One of the hardest things about running a business is learning how to make the best use of your time and your money. The time and money that are so easily frittered away can shock you when they're added up over a period of a few months. Cash flow problems often occur in new businesses when sales have been made, products have been delivered, and no one pays their bills on time. As a wholesaler, you can expect most accounts to pay from 30 to 60 days after you bill them, and that can be a long time if you're making payments to suppliers in the meantime.

Most experts will tell you to have at least a year's worth of capital to live on before you go into business, but you can make it with a lot less if you're prudent with your money and honest with your suppliers. Plan your budget long before you open your doors, and stick to it even when times are hardest. According to accounting experts, the major cause of bankruptcy isn't a poor cash flow, but the *thought* that cash flow couldn't be reconciled. Banks, suppliers, and leaseholders would much rather see you work out a payment plan than see you fail, which could result in a complete loss of their investment in you.

There are plenty of books, articles and business courses that will tell you everything you want to know about setting up and keeping a budget. (See Appendix A.) We suggest you read as much as you can about it, and talk to other business owners before deciding on your own method. Then think of everything that you'll have to pay for in the first few months of operation, including equipment, rent, public utilities, telephone service, supplies, labels, packaging, distributing costs, wages, office supplies, and bank charges. Next determine the amount of your product you'll have to produce to meet those requirements, and add 10 to 15 percent for unexpected expenses. Keep daily records of sales and purchases, and learn to amortorize your capitalization costs and set aside enough extra money each week to make monthly and annual tax and licensing payments.

Keep in mind that nothing teaches like experience. As Steve Bernstein says, "You know, people used to tell me, 'You're going to learn about cash flow,' and you can't learn about cash flow from reading a book! But when you're running a business, all of a sudden you go, 'Oh, this is what cash flow is all about.' " Still, you'll do a lot better by at least studying enough to know what to expect.

Time management is at least as important as cash management. Learning to budget your time for its best possible use will leave you a lot less harried and free up your family and amusement hours. A number of excellent books have been written on effective time management, and there are a number of tape recorded programs on the subject as well. (See Appendix A.) Here are just a few suggestions to help you get control over your time:

• *Decide which tasks are your highest priorities.* Although lots of people make lists of things to be accomplished in a given day, the tendency is to do the easiest things first. At the end of the day, a number of things have been crossed off, but often the most important projects are left undone. Being efficient is not enough—you must also be effective, and that means setting priorities.

• *Combine your errands.* If you're planning to make a sales call across town, schedule appointments with other companies nearby. If you shop for your own supplies, do it while you're already out, rather than making a special trip.

• *Make appointments.* Restaurant owners hate to be disturbed during peak hours and will send you away if you show up then with a new product to sell. Call first, and request an appointment at *their convenience.* You can usually schedule several appointments during a given block of time.

• *Plan for peak selling days or seasons.* If the weekend is your biggest selling time, gear up for it on Thursday and Friday by making enough of a surplus to last. By doubling his production on Fridays, Steve Bernstein is able to work a five-day week, and he can close on holidays and special occasions. With a little foresight, you can probably do the same.

• *Consider getting an answering machine for your phone.* It's hard to get things done when you're constantly running to pick up the phone. Because your friends know you're the boss, they may not hesitate to call you during peak production hours. By using an answering machine, you can save valuable time and still get your messages. This can be especially important if you're running your business from your home.

Growing Pains

One of the major reasons that new businesses fail is that they expand too rapidly. As production and capitalization costs increase, management skills often become too limited for the job and owners desparately try to make up for it by working longer hours and pumping more and more money into temporary solutions. Instead of working himself to death, a successful business owner will carefully control his growth and resist any temptations to try to become an overnight millionaire. As John Patton says, "Patience is the most important thing in a business. You want to grow real fast, and you want to be ambitious. You feel that if you don't go out and . . . change the world every day that ·you're not accomplishing anything. But unfortunately, you can't do that. You can't push. I don't know how it is, but there's a timetable for your particular product in your market area, and you can't push it faster than that timetable."

A good manager will know that timetable almost instinctively, and must learn to wait for the right moment to act decisively. "It's like a comedian on stage telling a joke," John continues. "Timing is everything. And the timing while you're waiting to take the next step is just excruciatingly painful, but you have to do it; you have to learn just to go with it."

Part of sticking to a good timetable is knowing your goal and constantly working toward it. By making good use of the telephone you can plan ahead for business growth and expansion without making commitments before their time. This is how John Patton puts it: "It's very helpful if you have any questions at all and you have a little bit of extra money to spend in any particular month to just get on the telephone and start calling around the country, asking questions like, "Who do you know that sells this kind of raw material in this state? Who do you know that sells packaging? Who does shipping? What are some names of distributors in other areas of the country? By building a network of information from around the country ˮor region where you plan to expand, you can begin planning each step toward attaining your business goal. As you start feeding information into your system, you can start narrowing it down and getting a picture step by step. You may not know when you're going to take that step, but you know that step has to be made. . . ."

The food wholesaling business can be used as a springboard for getting into a number of other businesses, and you may want to consider them as extra sources of cash as your company grows. Dionysos Heavenly Foods were so successful that they opened a small restaurant to serve their fancy Greek entrees and desserts. In addition, they cater to large parties, conventions and business lunches for a flat fee, and in the process gain many new converts to their Greek cuisine. When patrons from around the country began requesting Kansas City Masterpiece barbeque sauce, President Rich Davis responded with a mail-order service which now reaches across the nation and brings hundreds of vacationers to his retail and wholesale outlets each year. Other wholesalers have opened retail outlets and take-out stores. The possibilities are wide open when you have a good product line and growing consumer demand.

It's More Than Money

Some foodcrafters have made a fortune from their business. For others, the business merely provides a comfortable salary or a secondary income. But money isn't everything. As Steve Bernstein puts it, "I kind of like the fact that I'm doing it different than just about anybody else, and it's working! A lot of the things that have happened with the business are totally against every business rule—that's what's really neat about it." One of the things that continues to surprise him is the quality of employees the company attracts, and the fact that they consistently become not only an integral part of the working team, but close personal friends.

"I love the people who work for me," he said, "and they love me. You don't have that in a lot of businesses. They'll go out of their way for me because they know I'll go out of my way for them. It's . . . a family kind of thing."

Besides that, Steve enjoys the freedom and responsibilities of being his own boss. "The buck stops with you," he said. "You can't go to your supervisor and tell him something has to be done and let him take care of it. You're the bottom line."

There's something about taking an idea and seeing it develop into reality that brings out the best in people. The hard work, the long hours, the setbacks and occasional disappointments all seem to fade in importance when one sits back and looks at the accomplishments.

For some, the opportunity to learn valuable business skills and gain self-respect make it all worthwhile. This clearly was the case with Gloria Gilbert, who entered the business world with no experience to draw upon. "I've grown up a whole lot," she says. "The level of responsibility as a business owner is acute, and I don't shrink from it. I'm here. And that feels good." But Gloria's feelings of satisfaction aren't limited to mental growth. Recently she's begun thinking more about financial rewards and likes what she sees in the future. "Just recently I went on vacation and didn't even think about business for two weeks," she said. "It was just a luxurious situation. I said that I would like to have enough money to live like that; live like I was on vacation all the time. And a couple of days later, I realized I'm in the position to create that!"

For John Patton, the real rewards of foodcrafting are in learning and using a variety of business skills and creative energy. "It continues to give me a forum from which I can exercise my creativity to its absolute maximum in many, many areas," he says. For instance, "I can practice my biology; I can practice hard-nosed business; I can practice the marketing aspects of it. I think that's probably one of the most exciting things a human being can do . . . exercise his creativity. And this more than gives me a chance to do that."

Some Advice

Sometimes the hardest part of moving toward a dream is taking the first step. Starting a foodcrafting business can be risky, challenging, and tiring. It can test all of your resources before it gives you back the financial rewards you work so hard for. Yet when asked if they would do it all again, everyone we talked to replied that they would without a doubt. And as Alex of the Sons of Sicily says, "If you have an opportunity to do something like this, you may have reservations about it. You think it's going to be horrible, it's not going to work. . . . But then, if you don't do it, you might be kicking yourself for the next twenty years, saying 'Man, we could have made it!' "

Chapter 3
Creative Catering

Of all the cooking professions, catering is the most appealing to many foodcrafters. Every year, literally thousands of culinary magicians take their wizardry into private homes and banquet halls where they slice, dice, bake, flake, baste and taste for every type of special occasion imaginable.

The Appeal of Catering

Catering allows almost unlimited culinary creativity. If you can dream up a good-looking and good-tasting dish, you can almost certainly find appreciative palates for it in today's sophisticated market. In fact, in metropolitan areas where there is strong competition from other catering firms, restaurants, and freelance chefs, your company's success may lie in the original, exciting dishes you create on a day-to-day basis, a welcome activity if you love creating and testing recipes.

Catering is also one of the foodcrafting businesses you can start on a negligible budget. Although it's difficult or even illegal in some areas to do so, most caterers start their businesses in their own homes, adding equipment and cookware as needed and financing expansion entirely from profits. Since labor costs, rented equipment, supplies, and transportation expenses will be charged to your clients, your initial costs may add up to only a few hundred dollars.

Catering can be started part-time, a fact that, coupled with the low investment needed, makes it a very low-risk enterprise. You can accept and refuse engagements as you choose, and the typical nighttime and weekend hours required for most catered events make it perfect as a supplement to another job. Even as your business grows, you can fit your working hours to your own schedule. David Ziff, one of Manhattan's many independent caterers, allows himself a full month's vacation at least once a year (typically during the "slow" month of July) and often takes two to four additional weeks of vacation during the winter months.

Just because catering can be a low-risk business does not mean that only small profits are possible. If you stick to your budget and watch your profit margin, catering can be immensely rewarding. Though many caterers won't discuss their profits, others report an average profit of 30 to 80 percent of the total price of any given catered event. With costs of $10 to $200 per person, profits can quickly add up. John Fifield said, "It's the only thing I know of where you can make $3,000 to $4,000 in a one night stand."

The right combination of good food, excellent organization, and a good location have made millionaires of some caterers. Glorious Food, a twelve-year-old New York catering firm, grossed $5 million in 1981. Ridgewell, the venerable caterer to presidents and dignitaries in Washington, D.C., earned $8 million that year, and Chicago's largest firm, Gapers, topped them both with an income of $10 million. These are exceptional examples, of course, but they demonstrate the potential that exists for successful caterers.

Besides profits, there are other rewards in catering. Creating culinary masterpieces for brides, debutantes, actors and actresses, politicians, dignitaries, celebraties, royalty, and just plain folks can be rewarding in itself, and praise is often lavished on successful caterers. Some chefs have moved from the kitchen into the limelight of near-celebrity status themselves as their reputations have spread. It is not unusual for hosts to arrange their parties around the schedules of such celebrated caterers to ensure the party's success (and possibly, to enhance their own social status in the process).

Another appeal of catering is attributable to its non-commercial status. While restaurants, wholesalers, and food manufacturers may have to compromise quality to cut costs, a caterer's reputation depends on absolutely superior taste, and people are often willing to spare no expense in acquiring such quality.

Catering is more personal than many professions, and that has definite appeal for some people. While other foodcrafters may find it difficult to know their customers, catering is most successful when the caterer and client have talked at length, discussing food preferences, party plans, kitchen layout, and similar matters. Such business discussions are a necessity that often leads to pleasant social relationships and, occasionally, abiding friendships.

Finally, catering is immensely appealing to people who like being their own boss. "There's the good old American feeling about owning your own business," David Ziff said. "*You* control it. I think a lot of people have a feeling of powerlessness in corporations and places like that, but in catering, you control everything."

TALENT IN THE KITCHEN, MONEY IN THE BANK

Some people dream and plan for the day they can start their own catering business, but at least one person found himself unexpectedly involved in catering. David Ziff, a New Yorker who was bored with his exporting job in 1979, loved to cook but just laughed one day when a friend suggested he try his hand at cooking for hire. "At that time, when I thought of catering I thought of the whole bar mitzvah thing," he recalled. "It just wasn't something I seriously considered." But someone else did consider it, and the next morning David found himself tenuously established in his own catering business, a development that came as quite a surprise to him.

"It was my birthday," he remembered. "I was reading the morning paper and suddenly I saw this little ad that said 'David's Dinners—studied under Marcella Hazan, Diana Kennedy—specializing in French, French Provencal, Northern Italian cuisines . . .' and I thought, Well, that sounds like all the things I've done!" With mounting curiosity, David looked at the bottom of the ad and saw that, to his amazement, the phone number was his own.

The ad was a birthday gift from Alan Bell, the friend who suggested the day before that David try catering. It drew a limited response ("only four inquiries") but was the boost David needed to give catering a try. Working from his own small kitchen, David catered small parties and evening dinners, working around his full-time job and gradually building a clientele. There was never a big initial investment because he used his own cookware or rented special items, charging the expense to his client.

News of David's cooking abilities traveled fast. Within six months he had quit his exporting job and moved into a sparkling white kitchen in Manhattan. By then David Ziff Cooking, Inc., provided a full-time income for both David and Alan. Sales have doubled each year since then, and in 1982 revenues were over $200,000.

Discussing the outstanding success of his company, David said "When we first started out we didn't know anything about catering. Consequently, we had a fresh approach to all of it, and we came up with our own ideas." Creating his first hors d'oeuvres, for example, was more a matter of asking, "What can I make that's small and won't drip on the floor?" rather than copying the "typically catered things that you see in party after party." Using the same approach with all of his courses, David came up with dishes so distinctly different that rave responses from party guests came on a regular basis. "One of the great things about catering is the constant massaging of the ego that goes on," David admitted. "Sometimes, they'll call me out to take a bow and clap and do a toast to me," an occurrence that any caterer would appreciate. "I love having people tell me that I'm wonderful!" he said. "And with catering, you have people telling you how wonderful you are all the time."

Of course, there are times that catering is just plain hard work. A typical day finds David up and ready to work by 10 a.m., preparing the foods for that evening's engagement before packing it up for the trip. As he and his assistants work, calls come in for future jobs. Keeping careful notes, David marks off dates and plans menus, estimates costs and makes up grocery lists. By 4:30 he's ready to load the food into a waiting car and head for the night's scheduled party, where he often stays until early morning. All tolled, it comes to about 12 hours a day, seven days a week.

He gets a lot of help, though, from some "wonderful" employees, all actors and actresses who are young, spirited, and "too bright for their jobs." Trained to treat party guests with deference and efficiency, David's crew is also personable and conscientious, a fact that "makes for an easy working atmosphere." Some of them are hired on as servers, others as kitchen assistants, cooks or cleanup help.

As David's business grew larger, a system of organization became necessary. He and Alan split up the responsibilities at that point—a practice David recommends for other caterers: "Big caterers really need two people, one to do the cooking, the other to handle logistics. Otherwise it's just too much to handle." Now David does almost all the food preparation while Alan takes care of purchasing, hiring, bookkeeping, and client consultations. Alan also makes sure that large parties come off smoothly, as was seen at a recent dinner for 400 at Radio City Music Hall. "We had to create kitchens where there were no kitchens, prep areas where there were none, stairwells, and so forth." Alan did all that and also made sure that salt and pepper shakers were filled, silverware was properly placed, and extra napkins were within a short walking distance of each table. "It's an incredible logistical challenge" to organize such a party, David stressed. "You need thousands of items. It becomes very, very complicated, and you must be *very* organized." At that point, a partner or assistant becomes indispensable.

Besides the challenge of orchestrating hugh parties, David enjoys the "interesting and exciting people" that catering brings him into contact with. Most have "upperscale incomes" and consequently can afford his fees, which average $30 a person for sit-down dinners. Some are extravagantly wealthy. "I have a client who has a huge castle on an island off Long Island," he mused. "She raises her own pheasants, has her own vineyards, and has these incredible dinners in this hugh knight's dining room overlooking Long Island Sound. . . ." David has served dignitaries, politicians, actors and actresses, and even the Secretary of State there. Such dinner parties require impeccable etiquette and masterful food, and David strives to make each occasion unique by creating a new dish for each party: "You want the guests to have things they've never had anywhere else." The challenge of creating innovative, delectable foods for such people is exhilarating, he says, and well worth the long hours catering often requires.

Coming up with new recipes is, in fact, one of David's passions. Every day, he uses his background in a myriad of cuisines to create new combinations and blend new tastes. "I love . . . the tactile sensations, touching the food, working with it. I like going into an empty space and creating something." One of the nice things about cooking is the "immediacy of it," according to David. "There's the idea that when you start out to do something, you're done with it relatively quickly. The results are in in a very short time, whereas with most things people do, it may be a year or six months before they know [how it went]. With cooking you know right away. It just makes things very nice."

With all the cooking, planning, organizing and arranging, it might seem like catering is too complicated to be fun. Not true, David says. "I usually tell my clients that I probably have more fun in the kitchen than they have in their dining room!" The key ingredient, he says, is a love of people. "I'm great with people. . . . I love to be around them, make them feel good . . . that's important in catering."

David is justifiably proud of his business accomplishments and pleased to find that catering fits all his career needs. "At first I wasn't sure, cerebrally, how much catering could give me. But I found out there are a lot of challenges. You have to use your wits in catering. It provides you with both nerve-racking and very creative experiences."

IT'S NOT JUST FOR WEDDINGS ANYMORE

Catering has come a long way since the days when wedding receptions and bar mitzvahs were the main sources of business. Today, caterers are called on to create romantic candlelight dinners, breakfasts in bed for two, extravagant costume feasts, luxurious picnic baskets, exotic "theme" affairs, and dozens of other special occasions. Record sales figures are being set by caterers at a time when most other sectors of the economy are suffering from a stagnant economy.

Factors contributing to the growth in catering include a growing interest in and exposure to gourmet foods, the increase in two-income households, smaller kitchens and a growing awareness that relying on the special expertise of a caterer can be as justified as consulting a doctor or plumber for their special expertise. Perhaps the most important factor of all, however, is the growing demand for business catering. Glorious Food, a large and successful catering firm in New York, reports that customers such as Mobil Oil, American Express, Chase Manhattan Bank, and IBM are requesting foods that were unheard of a decade ago except on the finest of tables—and they're willing to pay up to $100 a plate to get them. Art Cohen, president of Gapers, Chicago's enormously successful catering company, flatly states that his company's livelihood depends on corporate patronage. In fact, top caterers across the country report that corporate business often accounts for as much as 70 percent of sales, a shot in the arm for a profession which seemed to be wallowing in a sea of wedding cakes and finger sandwiches only a few years ago.

Catering in today's market calls for a sharp business sense and a willingness to work hard. But for people with commitment and a creative flair, it offers one of America's best culinary opportunities.

OFF ON THE RIGHT FOOT

Before you print up business cards and jump into the catering fray, there are a number of things you should consider. This section discusses the skills necessary to make your catering venture successful, as well as some advantages and disadvantages of catering.

Are You Right For The Job?

As owner-operator of a catering business, you'll need to match your own skills to the job requirements, and that means honestly assessing your abilities and limits. If you don't have a particular skill needed for catering, you alone must determine whether it's worth learning or if you should hire someone else with the skill.

Caterers must possess a number of skills, the most important being organization. "You must be *extremely* organized to be successful at catering," David Ziff warns. With menus to prepare, food to buy, parties to plan, cookware to rent, and a hundred and one things to remember, good time management is absolutely essential. To plan his day, David writes a list of things to be accomplished on a large board mounted on his kitchen wall. He then arranges the list in order of priority, according to the sequence in which everything needs to be done, and assigns different tasks to himself and his employees. Because a caterer's day can be long and arduous, every time-saving technique helps.

Hundreds of would-be entrepreneurs begin their own catering companies every year, but far fewer succeed for an appreciable length of time. Part of the reason, David thinks, is the long hours and hard work. Many caterers work 10 to 16 hours a day during peak periods such as holidays and weekends. According to David, you have to be a "self-directed person" to work those hours, and you should consider the effect it can have on your family life. "It's easy to begin [a catering business] without much money, but if you're not really serious . . . it's going to be exhausting. You've got to love it! If you don't, and if you don't want to put a tremendous commitment into it, it's just not going to work for you."

A successful caterer not only loves the work, but loves the people. If he doesn't thrive on the excitement generated by the parties and social events he caters, he must at least appear to do so. He must be knowledgeable about current food trends and world events and be conversant on local affairs. The flexibility to go from a sorority brunch to a major political luncheon without missing a beat is required, and the creativity and imagination to create menus for these and every other occasion imaginable is needed.

A caterer's success often depends as much on his people skills as his culinary abilities. "Sometimes, if you haven't worked for her before, a hostess may be nervous about having you in her kitchen," David says. Pacifying nervous hosts and acting as maid, mother, nurse, psychiatrist, and marriage counselor may all fall in the range of roles played by a caterer. And where "executive affairs" are literal as well as figurative, discretion is imperative.

One of the unusual aspects of catering, according to David, is that "there's a whole gradation of the ways people treat you. Sometimes you're treated like just a servant, and other times you're treated like the great artist in temporary residence." Of course, the way you're treated often reflects the way you act. "If you act like a servant, they'll treat you like a servant, and if you act like someone special, they'll treat you that way." But, unlike most other jobs, catering allows for mutual testing: "Clients test me out, and I test them . . . , David says. "If I don't like them I don't have to work for them again, which is nice. Of course," he adds, "that's only happened with about five people in the past three years. . . . People [generally] treat you very nicely."

Some of the other characteristics essential to a successful catering business are:

• *Timeliness.* 6:45 may not be good enough for a dinner scheduled for 6:30, and such tardiness can have an effect on the amount of repeat business you get. Catastrophes aside, you should never be late.

• *Neatness.* The cleanliness of your cookware, equipment, kitchen, clothing, and your appearance will have a bearing on your business. Not only must you be organized, you must *look* organized too.

• *Frugality.* Without sacrificing quality, you'll need to keep a close eye on your budget. With the high cost of quality food and beverages, it's easy to go overboard, so be sure to leave an appropriate profit margin for yourself and keep within your estimated operating costs.

• *Thorough knowledge of proper etiquette, table arrangements, and traditions.* Hosts will expect you to know the appropriate table arrangements for each kind of service. In addition, expect any breaches of etiquette by you or your staff to be noticed. If you need to brush up on your social skills, visit the library and pick up a few books on etiquette, table arrangements, and social traditions, or take a class on these subjects at a culinary academy.

• *Presentation.* Presentation definitely influences the flavor of the food. Not satisfied with dishes which are merely attractive, some caterers use meats, pastries, condiments, fruits, and other foods to fashion exquisite sculptures and reliefs. In fact, food sculpturing has become so popular that full-length courses are now offered in it at some cooking schools.

• *Location of your catering firm.* The success of your business may depend to a large extent on the area in which you live. It's safe to say that people in New York are generally willing to pay more for fancy food than are people in Des Moines, and they may be more adventuresome in trying new foods. But you don't necessarily have to live in a big city to be a success; your catering firm can do well in a small town if you know the needs and wants of the people in your community and can supply them.

• *Fortitude.* As a new caterer, people may well balk at your prices. If you're convinced your prices are fair, stick to them. Too many caterers give "deals" to friends and special customers, without fully realizing all of the costs involved. Also, you will need to have the tenacity and endurance to carry you through "slow" times and seasonal fluctuations. Some of the other challenges you'll face are a capricious and sometimes extremely competitive market and clients with short tempers and (occasionally) unreasonable demands. Besides that, it's difficult to continue catering on a part-time basis for long. As David Ziff put it, "It's not something you can dabble in very easily. You may think you can limit yourself to one party a week, but it doesn't always work out that way. One week you may get six parties, the next week you may get no parties."

THE BRASS TACKS

Getting Legal

David Ziff and Alan Bell jokingly refer to New York City's many "underground" caterers as TBI firms—"Tasty But Illegal"—after the title of a newspaper article they read about the growing phenomenon of caterers operating from unauthorized kitchens. Most such firms are working from private homes, a practice which is illegal in many cities. To operate from an approved facility you may have to renovate a separate room in your home or rent another kitchen. Be sure the new facility is appropriately zoned, and check with your local health department about inspections. Among the requirements concerning catering which may be in effect in your area are the following:

- Local license to operate a food service company,
- Permit from the local health department,
- Local on- and off-premise licenses for preparation of food for public sale (an on-premise license is required only if you operate from your own banquet hall),
- State caterer's liquor license,
- Tax I.D. Numbers.

Insuring Your Business

A general liability and business insurance policy should be supplemented with a "floater" policy, which insures the equipment and cookware you take from place to place.

Finding a Kitchen

A number of options exist for renting approved kitchen space if it is illegal to operate from your home kitchen. Many restaurants, churches, and institutions use their facilities only during limited hours or seasons, and may be willing to rent their kitchen to you at other times. Because most of your cooking will be done during regular business hours, however, it may be difficult to rent kitchen space when you need it. If that is the case, you may be able to pool your resources with other caterers or food manufacturers (who often work from late night to early morning) or renovate your own kitchen space.

If you do remodel a rented space to meet health code requirements, choose a site that isn't zoned for retail uses. You'll pay much lower rent in warehouse or manufacturing areas. The quality of your kitchen, cookware, and equipment will have an effect on the quality of your food, however, so try not to sacrifice quality in your efforts to reduce expenses.

The Right Equipment

Because caterers transport food from place to place, special equipment and supplies are often required. You'll probably find that your needs will include the following:

- Ranges, ovens
- Chafing dishes
- Hot and cold boxes
- Cookware
- Linens
- Shelving for vehicle
- Freezers, refrigerators
- Serving supplies
- Pots, pans
- Paper and plastic supplies

As you grow in size you may want to rent or buy champagne

and punch bowls, wine servers, compotes, candleabra, and novelty items.

Most restaurant supply houses will rent cookware, dinnerware, serving pieces, and linens. The fees should be charged to your clients. However, be sure that the quality of the items you rent is up to snuff—plasticware and chipped dishes simply won't do for most occasions. The quality of the cookware you use can make a difference in the quality of your food, too. Establish a strict policy of promptly returning unacceptable items to the rental agency with a gentle note calling attention to their oversight. You'll soon be receiving only the best equipment and cookware from them (or else you need to seek out another rental company).

While some caterers buy service vans with elaborate shelving and storage boxes for transporting food, you can get by for quite a while with a good station wagon and styrofoam ice chests. David Ziff has found that he can fit about 800 cocktail party servings in his 1963 Comet, and rents vans or buses for larger events.

What Price Quality

Catering profits vary widely. To stay in business you'll need to ensure a consistent level of profit over and above your expenses. Among the expenses you'll need to consider are food and liquor costs, wages and salaries, equipment costs, rental costs, kitchen rent or lease costs, transportation expenses, and overhead such as bookkeeping, advertising, and other administrative costs.

Many caterers charge their customers directly for food, wages, equipment and cookware rentals, transportation, and similar items. You should clearly establish payment methods during your initial client consultation, and require a deposit at that time. Upon receiving a final cost estimate for the event, a client may pay up to 50 percent, remitting the remainder after services are rendered.

Advertising

Too many beginning caterers get off to a bad start with far too much advertising and not enough expertise. While giant newspaper ads and catchy radio spots can turn your business name into a household word, it can also break your budget. Most caterers rely on word-of-mouth advertising for the bulk of their business. As David Ziff put it, "We haven't advertised in years. We haven't had to! Most of our business is referral: someone will call up and say, 'I was at a party three weeks ago, and it was the best food I've ever eaten.' " That's the way it works for most successful caterers.

Still, you may need to prime the pump in the beginning before people have heard of you. The following are some low-cost advertising options to consider:

• *Free Samples.* There's no better way to advertise your expertise than to give away free samples of your best culinary efforts. Naturally you'll need to use some discretion in deciding who to give samples to, because the expense can quickly mount up. The trick is to make your samples available to as many of your targeted customers as possible without giving away a lot to those who wouldn't be likely to use your services. If you want to develop corporate business, for example, you might offer to provide a dessert tray at your city's next Chamber of Commerce function.

When you provide such free samples, be sure to leave a small stack of your business cards on a corner of the table. If people are really impressed with your samples, you'll be surprised at how many take a business card to keep you in mind for future events.

• *Fliers.* Fliers and circulars are very inexpensive, and you can distribute them yourself to churches, office buildings, libraries, and bulletin boards around town. They should be neat, creative, attractive, and give enough information about your services to encourage people to call for further information.

• *Professional Referrals and Reciprocal Name Trades.* Caterers often work out cooperative arrangements with other service professionals, including florists, photographers, bridal shops, bakeries, and gift shops. In making referrals yourself, really try to recommend the best service for the particular job. Try to name a specific individual for the client to contact, and ask him to mention that you made the referral. The other business will appreciate your recommendation and will reciprocate with referrals to you.

• *Direct Mail.* Using the leads from the businesses with which you've established reciprocal name trades, send letters (preferably handwritten) describing your services. Personalization is the key—standardized form letters will almost immediately be thrown in the trash.

• *Telephone Listings.* Don't just list your service in the Yellow Pages—take out a small block ad which describes your specialties and conveys your image. With competition from other caterers, restaurants and take-out stores, spelling out what you have to offer is vital, and people scanning the Yellow Pages looking for caterers will appreciate the additional information. Make sure your ad stands out from the rest!

• *Business Cards.* Business cards are inexpensive, and they represent your business to just about everyone you meet. Try to use the quality and creativity of your card to convey the image you want to promote, and include both your business and personal name, phone number(s), and specialties. You may also want to include a slogan and/or a logo.

PLANNING THE PARTY

The first step in planning a catered event involves getting to know the client's needs. If at all possible, a face-to-face consultation should be scheduled which includes a good once-over of the kitchen to be used. There are enough challenges in the catering business without, for example, arriving at a host's home to discover that the oven only works on the "broil" setting. The pre-party consultation should help prepare both yourself and your client for the party by carefully covering each of the following key areas:

• *Type of Occasion.* The reason for the event to be catered, as well as any theme around which it is to revolve, will have the most bearing on your menu plan. Try to learn as much as possible about dignitaries or guests of honor who are expected to attend. Serving their favorite dish or creating a new one especially for them may be appropriate and appreciated.

• *Type of service.* You should be aware that buffet meals generally require more food than sit-down dinners. This is not because people take more food at buffets, but because it's more difficult to guess the amount of specific foods people will eat at a buffet. While the number of steaks needed for a sit-down dinner is easily determined by the number of guests expected, it's hard to estimate the number of scallops needed to serve the same number of guests at a buffet.

• *Time of event.* Americans increasingly prefer lighter and fresher foods. "But for formal affairs," according to David Ziff, "they still want fancy foods, the heavier types of things." In general, the earlier in the day the event is scheduled, the lighter the food should be. After dinner events should also be light, but the type of occasion and food preferences of the client and guests will override any of your own guidelines.

• *Size of event.* The differences between a party for 20 and one for 200 will affect not only the amount of equipment, food, and labor you'll need to provide but the type of food to be served also. As the number of guests increase, so does the likelihood that some people will dislike certain spicy or unusual dishes, and it's your responsibility to come up with dishes that please the greatest number of people.

• *Food preferences, allergies, and taboos.* With so many people concerned about eating healthy foods today, you're likely to encounter hosts requesting low calorie, low salt, or low carbohydrate meals, and your ability to respond with foods that meet their requirements without sacrificing flavor will boost your value and reputation as a caterer. In addition, you should check for allergies, religious taboos, and personal preferences of your clients and their guests. Never try to force your own personal preferences on a host.

Some religions discourage or forbid the consumption of certain foods and beverages. This can apply to certain days of the week or year, or may be a lifelong taboo. Catholics often abstain from eating meat—but not fish—on Fridays, and the Jewish faith prohibits eating foods that aren't kosher, or approved by Jewish law. Meat is kosher if it has been bled and cleaned according to certain rules, and there are prohibitions pertaining to types of meat eaten. All shellfish, birds of prey, and pork products are forbidden by Jewish law, as is the mixture of meat and milk products. Mormon (Church of Jesus Christ of the Latter Day Saints) doctrine prohibits the consumption of caffeine (found in coffee, some teas, and some soda pops) and alcoholic beverages.

Many Eastern religions forbid the consumption of meat or certain types of meat, fish, and fowl. Other groups do not forbid the consumption of any food or beverage, but regional customs or preferences may dictate which foods will or won't be eaten. Most often, religious taboos and preferences involve the use of alcoholic beverages, meats, and substances that alter the natural state of well-being.

Be sure to check with your client for instructions pertaining to any religious restrictions.

• *Location of event.* Always visit the kitchen from which you'll be serving, or have a member of your staff visit it, being careful to note the following information:

> — *Type and condition of equipment:* Does the oven work on all settings? Is the refrigerator big enough to store everything for the number of guests and type of food you'll have? Do all range burners work properly? If a dishwasher is to be used for cleanup, does it require extensive rinsing before loading, and does it clean well? If using a banquet hall or convention facility, be sure to ask for instructions on dishwasher use. (Sometimes the facility will provide clean-up help and operate the dishwasher.)

— *Kitchen space available:* The size and arrangement of the kitchen may limit the menu possibilities, especially for larger groups. Be sure to ask the hostess or kitchen supervisor to clear all counters and create storage space in refrigerators as needed.

— *Cookware and cleaning supplies available:* Note the number and sizes of pots and pans, measuring items, serving pieces, cooking supplies and cleaning supplies available. Are there enough cutting boards? A complete dinnerware set for every guest? What about soaps, dishtowels and other cleaning needs? You'll need to supplement most of these items with your own supplies. Some hosts will allow you to use such staples as flour, sugar, salt, and so forth from their pantry, but you'll need to establish that beforehand and be sure that they have plenty of such staples available the day of the party.

— *Toilet facilities, entrances and exits:* Banquet halls and convention facilities will generally have separate toilet facilities for employees and guests, but private homes may not. Check with the host and, if possible, establish separate restrooms or agreed-upon times when it would be best for your help to use a central restroom. Also, the host may want you and your help to enter and exit from separate doors. This should be established long before the guests arrive and adhered to without exception.

— *Linens:* A host may chose to use his own tablecloths, cloth napkins, and other linens, or he may want you to provide them. Be sure there are enough linens for every guest and that they are cleaned and pressed the day of the event. Most banquet halls and convention facilities will provide their own linens but you may wish to have them pressed or bring your own higher quality linens for formal events.

Special linens include buffet cloths, lace covers and overskirts. Buffet cloths are usually one and one-half times the width of a normal banquet tablecloth and are primarily used for buffets. Lace covers may be used on buffet or banquet tables, and are especially attractive for formal use. Overskirts are placed around buffet tables and may be decorated with ribbons or flowers.

In addition to the above, you'll need some miscellaneous items such as potholders, hand and dishtowels, bar cloths and cleanup cloths. These may be provided by the host or you may wish to supply your own.

— *First aid:* If a first aid kit is not provided by the host kitchen, bring your own well-stocked kit, including sanitary bandages, burn ointment, smelling salts, and a first-aid manual. You and all of your employees should know how to use the "Heimlich Maneuver" in case food becomes lodged in a diner's throat.

• *Budget for the event.* In considering your host's needs you will develop a budget within which you'll be working. While some clients won't be concerned with cost until the final bill arrives, others will want to know how much everything costs at every step. If you can suggest cost-cutting methods for those concerned with cost, they'll be appreciative and be more likely to contract for your services again than if you shock them with an large bill in the end.

• *Logistics.* There are dozens of things to be considered before arriving at a host's house, chafing dishes in hand. It must be determined well in advance whether you or the host is responsible for purchasing the food, renting the equipment and cookware, and arranging for other services such as music, flowers, photographs, and so forth. Some hosts will want to handle all of it themselves and others will ask you to act as the party organizer and arrange everything for them. Be sure your estimated costs and final bill represent the full range of services actually provided, including consultation, arrangement of services, and rentals. If you require a minimum time limit for you service (generally four hours) the initial consultation is the time to say so.

• *Deposits and cancellations.* As a protection against cancellations most caterers require a deposit long before the scheduled event. This may run from only a few dollars to several hundred depending on the size of the group and the caterer's familiarity with the client. For new clients John Fifield charges a deposit of a dollar per guest, and others increase their flat fees according to the length of the guest list. Your policy on refunds should consider the amount of notice given for a cancellation and your ability to secure another event on that date. If you cater another party in place of the canceled event, consider returning the original client's deposit. The goodwill you will get from being fair will usually more than compensate for the money you lose by returning the deposit.

• *Cleanup.* Always leave a kitchen as clean as you found it, preferably even more so. One of the biggest reasons a host hires a caterer is to be able to stay out of the kitchen, especially during cleanup time. Banquet halls may provide help during cleanup or may put the cookware and dinnerware up after you've had them washed. If you rent your dishes and cookware, the rental company may do the cleanup (after a preliminary scrubbing). Be sure you know all cleanup policies with rental agencies, kitchen supervisors and hosts, and follow them to the letter.

After determining the needs of your client, it's time for you to figure the amount of food needed, number of waiters, bar help and cleanup persons to schedule, the number and type of decorations needed, and the time needed for food preparation. If you've contracted to arrange all aspects of the party, you should also contact each service required at this time, including florists, musicians, and bartenders (unless you provide your own).

Deciding on serving sizes.

The size of portions should be determined by the type of occasion, time and type of service, age and sex of the guests, and preferences of the host. Teenagers and young adults will typically eat much more than other groups; small children and senior citizens, the least. It will take some practice for you to quickly determine the amount of food people will eat, but these guidelines may help until you develop your own system:

• *Meats for sit-down dinners:* Children require 3 to 6 ounces of meat, depending upon their age. You can generally plan on 25 percent less than the same portion for adults. Teens and young adults need 8 to 14 ounces, adults need 8 to 12 ounces, and the elderly usually need 10 to 20 percent less than other adults, or about 6 to 10 ounces.

Buffet dinners, again, may require a slightly larger serving per person, and since the guidelines given are approximations, confer with your client about preferred serving sizes.

• *Hors d'oeuvres:* The number and type of hors d'oeuvres served should be determined by you and your client, but one caterer estimates that people eat four or five hors d'oeuvers during each of the first two hours and two to four per hour after that. Receptions and cocktail parties followed by a meal will require about a half to two-thirds that amount. The lightness of the hors d'oeuvres, the age of the guests, and the type of occasion will also affect the number eaten.

Hired Help

A dependable, efficient crew of assistants is vital to your catering success. Guests will remember a waiter's slip-up long before they remember the excellent food he served, and for that reason many caterers personally train each employee to reflect their own high standards. So sophisticated is one New York City firm that smiling is forbidden among servers, and those without a dish in hand must stand with their hands clasped behind their backs, in the tradition of servants to European aristocracy. David Ziff thinks such an approach is wrong for his catering firm: "People should feel that a *nice* person is waiting on them, but [the servers] shouldn't be chummy. What they're supposed to do is *not* call attention to their presence. They're trying to be as unobtrusive as possible, yet pleasant.'' His waiters and waitresses all have backgrounds in the theater and find the task easy. They work together as a cohesive team to make each guest feel pampered and relaxed.

The size of your operation and each party catered will determine the number and types of help you will need. Among the types of help most often used by caterers are chefs, first cooks, assistant cooks, pantry help, waiters and waitresses, bus help, bar help, cocktail servers and dishwashers.

Different types of occasions call for different numbers of servers, but a sit-down dinner generally calls for one server for each 10 guests. Plan on one bartender for each 50 guests. Cocktail parties may require one server for each 20 to 25 people, and trying to scrimp can create the danger of harried cocktail servers and irate guests.

Most caterers prefer to train their own help, but many agencies hire out waiters, waitresses, bus help, cleanup help and kitchen aides. In 1983 wages ran from minimum wage for less-skilled help to about $20 an hour for head waiters, often escalating on weekends and holidays. Fees for waiters and waitresses generally ranged from $5 to $17 an hour, depending on the size of the town or city and the nature of the catered event. Most agencies also charge a "placement fee" for their services: about $20 to $50 per party in 1983, although some charge a smaller initial fee and add extra charges for each helper placed.

Because the help you hire represents your business to the public, they should be neat, courteous, and efficient. Their uniforms should be spotless and well pressed, their hands clean and well manicured. Your employees advertise your values and business practices to every party guest. Make sure they understand the importance of their behavior and appearance.

Purchasing Food

Food purchasing is often a daily affair in the catering business.

The reputation of your business depends on quality and freshness, and mediocre food can quickly put you out of business. Many caterers prefer to buy their food from fresh food shops, farmer's markets and gourmet specialty shops. Costs are higher at these outlets than from wholesalers, but the risk of getting poor quality is greatly reduced.

Restaurant supply houses may be able to provide high quality staple items, however, and you may want to contact them for backup or bulk purchases (being sure to try samples of everything you order).

Theme Parties

Some hosts want their party to be so sensational no one will ever forget it. One California businessman, for example, contracted with his caterer to put together a poolside party at which topless waitresses retrieved live lobsters from the pool (drained and filled with seawater for the occasion) to be boiled in a huge cauldron. The caterer's fee was reportedly $39,000.

Other caterers have featured lions, tigers, and bears (handled by certified trainers, of course), sculpted foods, and waitresses dressed as slavegirls, gypsies, Hawaiian princesses, and countless other characters. If you're good at decorating and organizing such grand events, you'll love the creative leeway that theme parties give you.

EXPANDING YOUR HORIZONS

Catering can be rewarding and tremendously exciting for anyone who loves cooking and has a good head for organization. It can also be an inroad to success in other food businesses. Glorious Food, New York's famous catering firm, is considering a move into wholesaling specialty foods to department stores and retail outlets. If current negotiations are successful, it may also be one of the country's first franchised catering firms. If so, president Sean Driscall estimates yearly sales could reach $15 million by 1985.

Many caterers have gone on to become cookbook writers, specialty foodcrafters, cooking teachers, newspaper food critics and columnists, and restaurant owners. Others have stayed on in the catering business, building small enterprises into hugh, immensely profitable companies. There are few limits to what can be done in the catering field by creative, dedicated people.

Chapter 4
Mail-Order Foodcrafting

The food-by-mail industry serves a booming market, defying the slumping economy with an astounding growth rate and a burgeoning number of suppliers and customers—in 1981 the industry as a whole grossed $500 million, which averages out to an astonishing $1.2 million for each of its 400 firms.

The tremendous growth of mail order is due primarily to one factor: convenience to the consumer. Americans are finding that they can save time, travel expenses and the annoyance of pushing through crowded specialty stores by shopping through the mail.

As Tom Thompson, owner of C'est Croissant, a take-out and mail-order business in Allentown, Pennsylvania, expressed it, "I don't particularly like going to stores. I like the idea of just sitting down with the telephone, leafing through a catalog, calling in an order and receiving it a couple of days later. It's very simple, it's very efficient, and the prices are usually comparable to those in retail stores."

Besides convenience, mail order offers the consumer an amazing variety of foods to choose from. While a family in rural Arkansas may not be able to find rich Bavarian pastries in their local grocery store, they can order them from a Pennsylvania supplier and receive them, fresh and delicious, at their door in a few days' time.

In general, if your product is unique, is made of high quality ingredients, and is appealing to a recognizable segment of the population, you have a good candidate for mail-order sales. The trick is to analyze (and cater to) the interests of a large enough sector of the food-by-mail market to achieve a reasonable income.

Some of the products currently offered by mail-order companies include smoked meats and poultry, jellies, jams, sauces, fruits and vegetables, candy, pastry and confections, herbs, teas, coffees, pates, cavier, escargots and specialty seafoods. The Popcorn Factory in Illinois has tapped into the snack food trade by marketing its flavored popcorn through the mail, and Quelque Chose in Madison has profited by producing a nougat of Wisconsin cheese products covered with rich, creamy chocolate. Maple Grove has expanded its line of special Vermont syrup to include cheese and sausage, and L. Coffey, Ltd., in Minneapolis, markets its "Haute Canine" line as the "natural gourmet dog snack."

If you don't cook but do enjoy gourmet foods, look for regional specialties that will appeal to consumers in other parts of the country. At least a dozen Texas companies sell papershell pecans or pink grapefruit by mail, but there is also a market for Texas rattlesnake meat, froglegs, and Longhorn beef. A company in Edison, California markets specialty honey, and Maine businesses have long capitalized on their world-famous lobster. With a little imagination and a lot of determination, you can market a specialty food from your region in the same manner.

Advantages of Mail Order

Like any other business, mail-order foodcrafting can be entered with a splash. You can make a hefty investment in raw ingredients, equipment, advertising and elaborate packaging, and if you have lots of money to spend that's certainly a dramatic way to enter this lucrative field. But mail order is also one of the few businesses you can enter on a shoestring and, with a good product and sound management, "shoestring" mail-order foodcrafting can be developed into a solid, substantial enterprise.

Take Ben Stroheker's example. As Director of Marketing for a large candy company, Ben began to dream about creating the world's best candy. He became fascinated with the idea, asking friends and acquaintances to describe their idea of the ultimate candy. After thinking about the responses he had collected over an extended time period he began to notice some common denominators.

Working in the basement of his Massachusetts home Ben dabbled with chocolate, almonds, sugar and toffees before finding a combination he considered to be perfect. It was a chocolate-covered, almond butter crunch which he shaped into a sailboat and named "Sweet Sloop." Excited about his creation, Ben mailed descriptive fliers to the 75 people on his Christmas card list and placed a small ad in *New Yorker* magazine. The response was so encouraging that in 1975 the basement hobby was transformed into a full-fledged mail-order business. Ben added three more candies to his product line, found a few investors and became president of Harbor Sweets, Inc.

In 1982 Ben's company grossed a million dollars and employed over 150 people during peak seasons. With a 50 percent growth rate each year, Ben thinks his expansion potential is unlimited. Although Ben's success hasn't come without setbacks and disappointments, it illustrates one of the biggest advantages in the mail-order business: you don't have to have a million dollars to make a million.

The size of your investment will, however, largely depend on the nature of your product. Dan Rosenblatt and Charles Mount invested over $100,000 in their Salem, New York Menucha Farms smokehouse in order to meet government regulations for their smoked beef, pork and poultry. As a rule, meats are very expensive to process and market because of their perishability and the government regulations covering their processing.

The size of your investment will also depend upon the space and equipment needed to produce your specialty. Candies and cookies require less cooking and storage space than most pastries, cakes, and meats. If you can cook or process your food product in your home for the first year or so, you'll save a bundle in equipment costs and rented production space.

One of the most obvious advantages of mail order is the broad market it can reach. Tom and Mary Lynn Thompson run a small and successful croissant bakery in Pennsylvania. In 1982 customers began asking them to send their buttery pastries out-of-state and the Thompsons created the mail-order department of "C'est Croissant." Within three months of their first shipment the Thompsons had received orders from people in 48 states, a few foreign countries, and a crewmember aboard the U.S.S. Independence.

The Thompsons' investment in ads in a national food magazine paid off with a market that shows no sign of a slowdown. They were also pleased that they were able to project a rather elite, cultured image without the attendant inventory and "fancy fittings" a specialty retail store might require.

Because the Thompsons were accustomed to dealing with retail customers they were concerned about the effect mail order would have on customer relations. To their surprise they found that their company could grow through mail order without compromising the personal touch they enjoyed striving for. "It's not a face-to-face contact, but there is, nonetheless, contact both through the mail and over the telephone," Tom explained. "You can learn a lot about people without ever seeing them, we learned."

A mail-order business is also much less expensive to operate than a retail or wholesale business. Because you're eliminating the middleman and selling directly to the consumer, a higher percentage of profits can make it back to your pockets. Overhead costs are lower because you don't need an expensive rental space in a high-traffic area.

Your customers will also appreciate the freshness of your mail-order products. Retailers rely heavily on inventory and regularly push older products to the front of their store shelves. Your customers will receive your product a few days after shipping with a noticeable increase in freshness. Most mail-order companies guarantee freshness and replace any order without asking questions, and to be competitive you should too.

By marketing through the mail you'll also sidestep one of the most annoying retail and wholesale problems: bills that are paid late or not at all. By the time a wholesaler has received payment from a retail customer, 60 to 120 days may have elapsed. This is, in effect, a short-term, no-interest loan given to the retailer. Many a wholesaler has faced serious cash crunches because of this time lag. By dealing directly with your customers you will avoid this problem.

With a foodcrafting mail-order business you will generally require prepayment with your orders. By offering the option of payment by credit card, you can get some additional impulse orders, but you'll have to decide for yourself if the extra expense and paperwork is justified. Your banker can provide details on arranging for credit card payments.

Choosing the Right Product

You'll need at least one or two very special products to succeed in the mail-order foodcrafting business. New Canaan of Austin, Texas specializes in jalepeno and prickly pear cactus jellies. The Taos Chili Company of New Mexico is known for its tempting chili mix, and customers from all parts of the U.S. are delighted with the crawfish bisque, file gumbo and other New Orleans specialties they order from Creole Kitchens, Inc.

Like these, your specialty food product may be just right for direct mail sales. To determine how broad your market is you'll need to consider the following:

> *Uniqueness*—is your product really different, or at least the best available in a given category of foods? Don't expect advertising or fancy packaging to compensate for a product that's basically not high in quality or that offers nothing to distinguish it from the competition. If your product is the only one available that is made without preservatives, for example, you will have a distinct feature to help make you competitive.

Ease of Processing—although you don't want to compromise on quality, be sure you don't price yourself out of existence. Can you produce your specialty food without incurring prohibitive costs? Be certain that your target market can bear the costs of your food processing, with enough of a margin to ensure a reasonable profit.

Packaging and Shipping—will your pound cake remain visually appealing and full of flavor after packaging and shipping? Are your popcorn balls likely to lose their freshness after prolonged shipping delays caused by the Christmas rush? Remember that some products simply cannot be shipped without loss of quality or danger of contamination. To be completely safe, allow for up to ten days of widely varied temperatures and conditions during shipping, and judge your product's viability accordingly. (There are "express" shipment methods that are much faster, of course, but if you plan on using these you'll need a greater profit margin to cover the increased shipping costs.)

GETTING STARTED

Your local library may be your most valuable resource as you plan for your mail-order business. By locating books and articles on mail-order and food businesses, developing lists of trade associations and government agencies you'll need to contact, and thoroughly researching your competition you'll begin to develop an effective plan for your business. The amount of time you invest in research before committing money to your business can have a direct bearing on your chances for success.

There are a dozen or more books available on the subject of mail-order businesses, and they can provide valuable information about market research, ways to develop effective packaging for your product, techniques for writing advertising copy, and many other details common to any mail-order business. Trade journals can give you useful tips on everything from dealing with government agencies to selecting a computer when your business begins to really grow.

Your local Chamber of Commerce can be a source of valuable contacts within your community. At some point you may need to consult a lawyer, accountant, advertising consultant or other professional, and knowing who has the best reputation for effective troubleshooting can be worth a lot.

The Direct Mail Marketing Association is another good source of information. Local members may be especially helpful in steering you away from common mail-order mistakes and in providing you with names of local government officials you'll need to contact. They may be able to help you find the equipment needed to process your product, give you tips on finding space for rent, and help you to find the right kind of employees or partners for your business. They may also be able to tell you which mail-order businesses have failed and which have been most successful.

You need to thoroughly research your competition, packaging for your product, equipment availability and costs, shipping, and advertising. Chuck Chase, president of Pacific Coffee and Tea Co., Inc., looked through back issues of food magazines, trade journals and regional publications to learn all he could about his competition. He noted that small companies offering certain items came and went, indicating the lack of a viable market for those products. He also noticed an absence of catalogs offering a wide selection of gourmet items, and he now produces a catalog of over 500 specialty foods and cooking ingredients.

By the same process of checking ads in magazines and newspapers you can gauge the strengths and weaknesses of your competition. Is your product sufficiently unique and different from theirs? Is the quality of your product comparable, or preferably, better than theirs? Are their advertisements targeting the right market or can you find a more appropriate (and lucrative) niche? You may want to order competitive products to find out about your competitors' shipping methods and effectiveness, quality of packaging, and taste.

Equipment and Kitchen Space

To learn which equipment and cooking utensils will result in the most consistent product quality you should study catalogs of commercial cookware suppliers. The equipment you need may be available secondhand from a restaurant supply company, or you may be able to lease what you need, thereby greatly reducing your capital outlay. Check your newspaper for equipment sales and bankruptcy notices for especially good bargains. Don't be afraid to bargain with suppliers—they're used to it and it can save you money.

Are you planning on doing your foodcrafting out of your home? It can save you money to do so—especially when you're just getting started. You'll need to discuss this with your local health department, however, and you may discover that it simply isn't feasible.

Elk and Moose lodges, American Legion halls, cooking schools, universities, public school home economic classes, churches, and restaurants and bakeries have kitchens that sometimes go unused. You can often rent such kitchen facilities when they're not in use and the health department will be much easier to deal with if you use a previously approved kitchen.

Packaging

Finding the right package and the right graphics for your product may be one of your most critical tasks. You may find that packaging your jam or honey may be as simple as covering a glass jar lid with a pretty calico and gluing on a label. Or you may, like Bonnie and Clyde Ice Cream Shops, hire a packaging house to decorate special tins with old-fashioned art work and bright colors (not for ice cream—they sell popcorn in these tins by mail). Your pocketbook is going to have a major bearing on deciding which options are right for you.

It's important to keep in mind that your package is the first thing your customer will see. You want the label, colors, style and outer packing to represent your company's image favorably. A trip to your local grocery store should convince you that packaging is one of the most important aspects of sales. It's clear that sales can be lost because of ineffective packaging or advertising, although a good mail order product can help make up for a less-than-perfect package providing the product arrives undamaged. Nevertheless, an attractive and functional package will portray your company as one that pays attention to details and cares about public image.

Your package must not only be attractive, it must also perform well in shipping. Adequate packaging is especially important when glass jars, fragile pastries or liquid products are involved. To test a package's performance, mail a few samples to friends or relatives in different parts of the country. This is a good way to get feedback on the freshness of your product, too. You may want to include a short questionaire asking your friends to evaluate the product and package in terms of durability, effectiveness and attractiveness. To find the package that is most cost-effective and durable may require experimenting with a number of different packages in this way.

One thing you'll want to do is include a descriptive label or small card in the package detailing ways in which the product can be used, giving cooking and storage instructions, and maybe giving a history of your product or your company. Some foodcrafters include recipes along with their products, and this can be especially effective as a way to introduce ethnic or regional foods.

Shipping

When your product leaves your location it passes through the hands of many people who may or may not be conscientious in their work. Check your local shipping companies carefully both for prices and guarantees covering lost and damaged parcels before committing yourself to any one of them. The extra costs some of them may charge could mean the difference between satisfied and disappointed customers, with obvious effects on your business.

Pricing

In order to determine the price of your products you should calculate the cost of your raw ingredients, rent, insurance, labor, equipment and other costs. Most mail-order businesses then double that figure (thereby making a 50 percent profit) for retail sales. Marketing and administrative costs are usually deducted from the gross profits, however.

Some items are very expensive to produce, making a 50 percent profit unreasonable. You'll have to use your best judgment in deciding the value of each product. Menuchah Farms makes little profit on their smoked filet mignon, but they feel the item is so special that they continue to produce it, counting on their other products, with larger profit margins, to make up the difference. In retail terminology, such a product is known as a "loss leader," and is often the key to successful promotion strategies.

Once you get to the point where you are developing catalogs on a regular basis, pricing becomes more complicated. John Gibbons of Harringtons has to price his November catalog in late July by guessing what the economic conditions and prices of ingredients will be several months in the future. "It's difficult," he said. "We use government reports, we use reports from our suppliers, and then finally we just have to guess.

"Some years we guess right," he said, "and some years we don't."

Labor Requirements

Between 40 and 75 percent of all mail-order business occurs from October to January. The jump in labor requirements can be staggering: one company adds 1,400 people to its permanent crew of 200 during this period.

Your labor needs obviously won't be this great as you start out, but they could change just as drastically when the holiday season rolls around. Not only will you need to be geared up for the increased demand at this time of year, you'll need to train a new group of employees and have the funds available to pay them. Having a reliable, permanent team will be a tremendous help as your temporaries learn the ropes. Although you could probably get away with paying minimum wage, you may be better off in the long run by paying a bit more to secure the loyal help that can see you through hectic times of peak demand.

Insurance

Although the chances of your product spoiling in transit are slim, one episode of food poisoning could mean a lawsuit and the end of your business. You should protect yourself with a good general liability policy, and you may want fire insurance and theft insurance as well. As with most business services, it pays to shop around when contracting for insurance coverage.

Legal Considerations

One of the most confusing and frustrating aspects of opening (or running) a business can be the government regulations covering all phases of production, packaging and marketing. Regulations will vary greatly with the type of food you're producing, the equipment used, and the city or state where you're located. Some mail-order business people operate safely and effectively out of their homes, but for many others government regulations make this impossible.

When Dan Rosenblatt started smoking turkeys with fruitwood at Menuchah Farms, he knew that there would be some government regulations to deal with. A year later, he had invested $100,000 in special flooring, special knives and cutting boards, special sinks and even a special type of road leading into the smokehouse. While the government inspectors told him all this was to be done to protect the consumer, they also told him how much water he could legally inject into his poultry to boost profits (a practice Dan has steadfastly avoided).

There are many stories about businesses spending enormous amounts of money to bring a location up to par with one set of government regulations, only to later find that the work must be redone to fit another set of regulations. The point is to be sure to cover all bases by working with all government agencies involved before you commit money to your project. It could save you a lot of money and headaches further down the road.

TARGETING YOUR MARKET

Advertising

To a large degree, the success of your mail-order business will depend on your effective use of advertising. The key word here is *effective*: it's all too easy to go overboard with a media blitz which does little more for your business than to put you quickly in the red. To start out on the right foot you'll need to concentrate on targeting your market.

Until a few years ago, targeting the gourmet food mail-order market wasn't so easy. Companies depended largely on women's home magazines, random mailings and rented lists to market their goods. There were no guarantees that any of the recipients were particularly interested in gourmet or specialty foods.

Thanks to gourmet food and cooking magazines, targeting the specialty food market is much easier today. Such publications as *Bon Apetit*, *Gourmet*, *Cuisine* and *Cook's Magazine* reach hundreds of thousands of readers with a demonstrated interest in fine foods.

A small ad in any of these publications can reap impressive results, although their advertising rates are not cheap. Expensive ad rates for such publications can be justified, however, because their readers are specifically interested in cooking and eating specialty foods and often have the economic ability to experiment with new products or splurge on foods for special occasions. The thing to remember about ad rates is that they are directly related to the number of readers. Thus a publication with very low ad rates may not necessarily be a bargain—because it's the cost per reader, and the *type* of reader, that count.

"My hunch is that there are three types of consumers," Ben

Strohecker of Harbor Sweets said. "Obviously, the first are the people that are used to having the best regardless of cost and have enough money to always buy the best. The second group does whatever the first group does; they don't know why, but they do it anyway.

"And the third group is my favorite group," he said. "My favorite group are the people who know the best. They perceive the value of quality. They don't always have the money to buy the best but they save their pennies and make it a very special occasion when they can."

Of course, effective promotion of your business will not always depend on expensive advertising in slick periodicals. When Harbor Sweets introduced their first candy, for example, Connie Strohecker told her friends about it in a personalized note:

Dear Friends:

"Sweet Sloops" are the result of a challenge to make the "best piece of candy in the world."

Ben told me that most candymen claim a homemade almond butter crunch covered with chocolate is the best combination they know, but they sadly admit that it is impossible to make commercially because of the fresh butter and all of the handwork required.

So with cookbook combinations of *Fanny Farmer*, *Better Homes* and others, our kitchen stove rewarded us with some pretty good candy.

A shortage of dark chocolate one Sunday afternoon forced us to try some white milk chocolate coating on the triangular crunch. "Sailboats," Ben Jr. said when he saw them. "Sweet sloops," I said, and our sweet fleet set sail.

Friends and neighbors asked if we wouldn't please pack a few boxes for them to use as presents, so we did.

Ben Sr. said, "Why be selfish with your discovery—tell your friends,"—So I am!

    Love,
    Connie

You can bet that a letter like that got a warm response, and the Stroheckers have kept up the friendly image in their brochures, catalogs, and correspondence with their customers.

With increasing numbers of people becoming interested in gourmet foods, the results you get from experimenting with different media may be well rewarded. Regional magazines, newspapers, and television stations have proven successful for some companies, although the danger of overloading on the number of media you use is something to watch out for.

If your product is made without preservatives or artificial ingredients, *The Mother Earth News* or other publications aimed at "natural lifestyle" readers can be especially effective. Restaurant and specialty food trade publications can be effective for certain types of products, and they can also provide you with information about methods of advertising that have worked for other companies.

In order to determine which publications best fit your needs, write to a number of different ones and request demographic and pricing information. This will give you the age, income levels, regional concentration, sex, and number of subscribers that the publication reaches, as well as the cost for various sizes of ads. Determine which publications reach the largest numbers of your target market for the least cost, and then keep careful records of your test ad results. It is always safer to test with small, relatively inexpensive ads before taking the plunge with full-sized, expensive ads that may not "pull" the responses you expect.

A relatively new and potentially profitable advertising medium is cable television. Some gourmet mail-order businesses have already tapped into this burgeoning medium as new, specialized channels are created.

It will probably take a while for you to determine which media are the most cost effective for your products. It will require meticulous record keeping as you try different approaches with different media and compare the results. As John Harney of Sarum Tea Co. advises, "Think of who your market is going to be, how wide it is. . . . You've just got to keep trying until you get your winning formula, and when you reach that winning formula you've got to press with it."

Public Relations

Your very best advertisement is unsolicited: the satisfied customer who tells his neighbor about your products; the newspaper or television food critic who features your specialty in a feature; the magazine that includes your company's name in a specialty food article. All of these can add substantial new business without any investment other than your product's high quality and unique appeal.

Publicity can do so much for your company, in fact, that advertising can become secondary. Dan Rosenblatt and Charles Mount didn't advertise for years after newspaper articles raved about their smoked poultry and meats. A local news story about Roy and Gail Cohn, owners of the Bonnie and Clyde Ice Cream Shops, was picked up by the national newspaper chains, television stations and magazines, bringing letters and orders from all over the country. Articles in gourmet food magazines have resulted in a flood of inquiries to many mail-order firms, sometimes doubling or tripling their sales volume virtually overnight.

Your job as far as public relations is concerned is to get the attention of the people who can tell your story. A dramatic background brought Roy Cohn national attention: as an ex-convict who worked against heavy odds to make his mail-order popcorn business successful, he earned the respect and admiration of many thousands who read or heard about his background.

To get national attention, people have tried all manner of gimmicks and bizarre publicity stunts. Some of these may work for a time, but your best bet is to let those people who can publicize your business taste your product and judge for themselves the quality and uniqueness that you're selling.

Tom and Mary Lynn Thompson thought their croissants were worthy of special notice and, following the advise of a friend in advertising, mailed gift packages to 100 food editors across the country. "The play we've gotten from it," Tom said, "is, well, pretty amazing. We have people calling from all over. We've gotten a lot of free advertising, and better advertising than you can pay for! When a newpaper editor gives you editorial mention, it swings a lot more weight than a paid advertisement."

There are dozens of ways you can publicize your products without a large outlay of cash. Regional and local food fairs, bazaars, bake sales, and civic activities will expose your products to people who may want to buy them for gifts or for themselves. You might demonstrate your food at a local cooking school or cookware shop. Be sure to take along promotional literature, and remind people that you can mail their gifts for them.

You may be able to have your product included in a catalog put out by a large national mail order merchandiser. This will bring you an immediate market, although you will have to split your profits with the catalog company. You can develop a list of likely catalogs from directories at your public library, and then simply write the Purchasing Director of each catalog and include a sample of your product.

National Food Fairs

An effective way to meet food editors and prospective customers is by attending national food fairs. Twice each year the National Association for the Specialty Foods Trade (NASFT) displays an amazing variety of gourmet meats, condiments, desserts, cheeses, and other foods and beverages. By exhibiting your specialty food in one of these shows you'll expose your products to hundreds of people in the gourmet food trade.

The results can be phenomenal. Soon after the Cohns designed special tins for their flavored popcorn they entered a NASFT fair. "All of a sudden," Gail said, "everybody just went crazy. They just really loved it," she said with a laugh, and orders began pouring in. By investing a few days' time, travel expenses and fees for a rental booth, the Cohns gained an instant national market and valuable business contacts.

PROMOTIONAL LITERATURE

Brochures

Descriptive brochures can be a handy means of reaching selective markets when you have only a few items to sell. You will want to include mouth-watering descriptions of your products, prices, your logo, address, phone number, order form and some type of art work. A professional photograph of your product can be expensive; as an alternative, you might try a simple drawing.

Decorative borders, stylized typefaces, and upbeat copy can add charm and interest to your brochure. You'll want to add emphasis by using bold type, testimonials, and lots of "white space"—too much straight copy will cause your readers to lose interest. Your local library can help you, once again, with books on advertising and graphic design.

Brochures can be hand- or typewritten and printed at a relatively low cost if you don't require a lot of color work. This doesn't mean that to be inexpensive your brochure has to be printed in black ink on white paper, however. A colored ink on a contrasting color of paper can be very effective and still be resonable in cost. It's when you require more than one color of ink —which usually means more than one run through the press—that costs will quickly mount.

You can save on envelopes and postage by using your brochure as a "self-mailer." This simply means that you leave one side of your brochure blank for addressing, allowing you to forego an envelope. By sorting your mailings by zip code and mailing at least 200 pieces at a time you can qualify for bulk-rate 3rd class postage and save money.

As you expand and grow you may want to consult marketing and advertising experts. Their expertise is not cheap but they can do wonders for the appearance and effectiveness of your promotional literature.

Newsletters

Some mail-order firms print newsletters complete with recipes, regional history, information about the company and friendly patter. John Beck's Buffalo Bulletin, from Beck's Sausage in Wyoming, is printed on newspaper stock with wide margins and includes informal drawings and lots of humor in a colloquial writing style.

One issue featured a recipe for Tucker's Stew for an army of 3,937. Two large buffalos were called for: "Cut the buffalo into bite-sized pieces. This will take about two months. . . ."

The goal of such playfulness, of course, is to form an easy-going, personalized relationship with your customers. Once your customers feel like part of the family you'll have developed loyalty and repeat business.

If your image is more cosmopolitan than folksy, set the tone of your newsletter accordingly with less homey grammar, more precise margins, professional art work, a finer typestyle and a better grade of paper. Your image will, to a degree, determine the type of people who buy your products. Keep your promotional literature consistent with the image you want to project so that your customers can easily recognize and identify with your communications.

Catalogs

As you add new products to your line you'll eventually want to develop a catalog. Clearly a full-color, magazine-style catalog is more desirable than a black-and-white pamphlet, but the cost can be astronomical. Catalog printing and mailing costs are two of the largest expenses many mail-order companies face. Unless your budget is especially large you'll be better off waiting until your product line includes about 50 items before attempting a full-color catalog. Professional marketing help is strongly recommended at this stage.

Mailing Lists

The development of a productive mailing list is a continuous job that will require organizational abilities and close attention to detail. Although you can rent mailing lists from numerous firms, most specialty food mail-order businesses we talked with found them to be ineffective.

A much better approach is to develop your own. Every time you receive an order from a new customer you've got a new addition to your in-house list, and experience will probably show that promotional mailings to this list will be at least twice as effective as mailings to any other list you might acquire. Eventually your in-house list will become one of your most valuable resources. It will be well worth the effort to keep it up-to-date and free of duplicate names.

You should stay alert for other sources of names, too, however. Alix Vandivier of Creole Kitchens, Inc. consulted her Chamber of Commerce and now receives a weekly listing from them of people who have written requesting information about New Orleans. Ben Strohecker found that his Christmas card list brought regular customers whose special interest in his business prompted them to recruit other customers.

Your church or civic organization might lend you its mailing list, or you might have luck with lists borrowed or rented from cooking schools, caterers, or specialty food stores in your area. Your very best advertising is word of mouth, so definitely encourage satisfied customers to recommend the names of friends who might like your product. Developing a really effective mailing list is a long-term proposition, so be patient, but be consistent in working on it.

It is vitally important that you keep track of the responses from your promotional efforts both in order to build your mailing list and to judge the effectiveness of your various promotions. Keep a copy of every name and address to which you send information. Eliminate those that are returned to you with no forwarding address. You may want to mail at least three times to the same non-responding address before crossing the name off your list, and more times than that if your budget can stand it. Some large companies mail up to a dozen times before considering a prospect hopeless: a general rule of thumb in advertising is that people may see an ad seven times or more before taking positive action on it.

Coding the order form (such as "C1" for the first mailing to your Chamber of Commerce list, "X" for your Christmas card list, and so on) will quickly peg the most receptive groups on your lists so you can single them out for more intensive promotional efforts. Develop reliable records for this as well as the products each customer orders, the amount of money they spend, when they buy and the form of advertising that introduced them to you. It's easy to let all of this information get out of hand, so do the paperwork as a daily or weekly routine. Any system you choose to use will work if it allows you easy access to the information.

Satisfied customers who repeatedly order your products will become your major source of income. This type of steady, repeat business must be gradually built through producing a quality product, using functional and attractive packaging, and developing the habit of doing what's best for the customer. This may occasionally cost you in merchandise, shipping, and sometimes in pride, but the reward will be loyal repeat business.

One of the best things that you can do to encourage repeat sales is to make your customers feel as if they're part of your family. The Stroheckers do this by using a familiar, almost intimate tone in their handwritten catalog. In one instance, while promoting a popular book about chocolate in their expanded mail-order catalog, they wrote "We've learned that not everyone has it (my mother doesn't have it, for example, nor does my cousin Wendy.)"

That kind of personal tone sets the scene for healthy customer relations, and, backed with a conscientious attitude and attention to the customers' needs, has made many friends and a good livelihood for the Stroheckers.

Personal Characteristics Necessary for Success

The mail-order food business can be decidedly lucrative, with the demand for high-quality, unique specialty foods being nearly unlimited. As in any business, however, many have failed at mail-order foodcrafting. The failures are usually due to improper management, disorganization, or lack of commitment. A common theme which comes up in interview after interview with successful foodcrafters is the absolute necessity of persistance, commitment and dedication on the part of anyone wanting to enter this field.

Ben Strohecker believes that for a person with these qualities, the sky is the limit. "For somebody to go into something like this that they've only been thinking about and dabbling in is a guaranteed failure," he said. "But if somebody loves their idea so much that they're willing to stay up half the night to perfect it, and their sights are set on their dream, and they're committed to their dream, they'll be successful."

There are countless examples to back up Strohecker's observation. Alix Vandivier of Creole Kitchens remembers her discouragement when twelve banks turned down her request for additional capital (backed by an entire book she had written about the business and its potential.) Another person may have given up the idea as hopeless, but Alix recognized the demand for her Creole specialties and searched for other sources. Eventually two loyal Creole Kitchen customers put up private funds and bought into her business, injecting the needed lifeblood to allow her fledgling company to grow.

Ben Stroehecker faced financial problems when his employers anticipated his move into his own full-time mail-order business and forced him into it six months earlier than he had planned. With no collateral or equity, banks and venture capitalists wouldn't touch his project. Without the strong commitment Stroehecker had to his idea and the assistance of "angel" friends who invested because of that commitment, Harbor Sweets would probably never have become the success story it is today.

Your Business Sense

A good business sense is essential to the success of your operation, as are attention to detail and organization. If you're great with people but a disaster when it comes to dealing with numbers, you may want to consider finding a partner with the type of abilities you lack. Someone has to be able to handle the numbers side of this business, just as in any other type of business.

If you're going to do your own bookkeeping you may want to take a course in general accounting. It should cover taxes, payroll, income statements and balance sheets. Although you may be able to accomplish a lot on your own, you'll need an accountant for year-end taxes and general financial advice. An alternative to doing your own bookkeeping is to have it done by a computer firm that specializes in small business bookkeeping. The fee is usually reasonable, and the time it saves can often justify the expense.

Organization and attention to detail are basic characteristics of a well-managed enterprise. A quick response to a returned order, personal notes enclosed with repeat orders, friendly telephone manners and quick access to a customer's records will bring you valuable goodwill and repeat business.

PLANNING FOR THE FUTURE

Computerization

It won't be long before computers are as common in American households as television sets are now. Some authorities are predicting that retail stores will become less important as people flip through video catalog "pages" and choose the items they want to buy.

Whether or not retail stores become obsolete, your business as a mail-order firm is ideal for computerization. Larger companies are already gearing up for this exciting new marketing method. You'll increase your competitiveness in the marketplace by learning everything you can about computers and how your business can use them to market your goods.

In the meantime, computers are becoming essential in business as a means of processing and retrieving information. Alix Vandivier made a hefty investment in computer equipment before beginning her mail-order business and found, after five months of operation, that the computer was doing the work of eight people.

As computers become less expensive and more "user friendly" they will become more and more useful for your mail-order operation, and ultimately they will be indispensible.

Expansion

Ben Strohecker began Harbor Sweets with one very special candy made in his home, and soon expanded to three other varieties. His catalog still features the four candies, but also includes twenty other specialty items as spinoffs of his nautical theme. You can now order twenty "Sweet Sloops" delivered in a picnic basket, or a brass boat horn filled with the chocolate goodies. Coffee mugs are decorated with renditions of sailboats and filled to the brim with the chocolates. Special gift items are available for Christmas, with appropriate packaging and gift cards.

You can be as creative as you want when you add new products: they may simply be a variation of your regular products, or something entirely different. By sending along samplers (in specially made, smaller containers) with each order, your customers can taste your new product without risk or obligation on their part.

Another possibility for expansion involves specially commissioned jobs. Ben Strohecker made his first special sale to the Boston Museum of Fine Arts—a chocolate-covered "mummy" hidden in a pyramid-shaped package in tribute to the museum's popular Egyptian collection. It was so popular that the museum ordered another line: miniature candy hard-hats in celebration of the opening of a new wing of the museum. Soon he began getting orders from other important clients, including the U.S. Constitution Museum, Boston Symphony Orchestra, Sheraton Hotels, and the Children's Museum. Wholesaling to gift shops and other outlets now comprises about 30 percent of Ben's total business.

Your growth won't necessarily be limited to adding additional products, either. By exhibiting their products in local bazaars and food fairs, some mail-order businesses have built up such a large local market that they eventually opened retail outlets, or began wholesaling to specialty food stores and supermarkets. People may ask you to cater a party with your smoked meat, or supply a convention with your French pastries. Your continued growth can depend on your ability to watch for such opportunities and respond accordingly.

Whether or not you want to expand into other food service areas, a mail-order business can be an exciting, rewarding opportunity for you to be your own boss in the gourmet food industry.

Chapter 5
Cooking Classes and Schools

There's no doubt about it: cooking schools are flourishing as Americans develop a taste for new and unusual foods and become less willing to settle for bland, uninspired meals. Media exposure to the cultures and cuisines of other countries, a generally higher level of affluence, and an enormous jump in travel since World War II have helped create a society of people who are seriously interested in experimenting with foods and generally more sophisticated about cooking. European, Oriental, Latin and other cuisines are becoming increasingly popular, and lately an interest has developed in a "back to the heart of America" group of simple but innovative American foods.

People are now ready, even eager, to try foods they hadn't heard of only a few years ago. This new interest in varied cuisines, together with the high price of eating out and an increasing interest in home entertaining, has resulted in a ready market for a wide spectrum of cooking classes.

If you can cook and you're good at teaching, you can make money by sharing your expertise with others. Whether you teach those in your neighborhood to bake flaky croissants on a strictly informal basis or open a full-time school of Chinese cuisine, cooking classes are an excellent way to tap into the booming gourmet food industry.

The Experience of Others

Peter Kump had taken innumerable cooking classes himself before ever thinking about teaching. "I kept going to these classes," he recalls, "and I was surprised to find that the instructors didn't know as much as I did—some of the very basic things about cooking! So I started asking myself 'What would be the most concise way to teach people to cook?' "

He began toying with the notion of teaching "more as a hobby than anything," and six weeks later had written a five-week beginner's course in French cuisine. He gathered a small group of friends (who had often asked him to teach them his techniques) and turned his Manhattan kitchen into a nighttime classroom. Word-of-very-gratified-mouth soon filled a second, then a third class, "and it just went on from there."

That was in 1974. Peter had a full-time job, so his cooking classes were only a sideline. By 1975 the classes had outgrown his small townhouse and he began searching for a larger location. Eventually he found an apartment on New York's East Side which had been home to a series of cooking schools and featured white walls, white tile floors, ovens, ranges, and a central work table with cutting surfaces. Peter's total investment for his new location was "nothing": a month's rent and the purchase of a small convection oven. Because New York City had no zoning or health restrictions on cooking schools, he wasn't required to be licensed or have inspections. He did his own bookkeeping and was covered by the insurance of the apartment's leaseholder.

The Peter Kump New York Cooking School started in its new home with two classes a week, still a part-time business for Peter. Today, Peter sometimes works 60 hours a week as director of the school, which grossed about $120,000 in 1981 and registers several hundred students each year. The school has expanded from the initial five-week participation class to include four other courses in a progressive program, complete with exams, that will transform a novice cook into an expert French chef. ("And," said Peter, "we make everyone start at the bottom. I don't care if you're a cooking teacher, you can't get into an advanced class without going through the beginning!")

At $295 per five-week session, the classes draw such devoted students that one woman commuted weekly from her Florida home, while others have taken the same class four times. Two additional instructors and four classes were added in the spring of 1982, bringing the total to nine classes a week.

The school has been a catalyst for other ventures: Peter hosts at least one gastronomic tour a year and is chef on two cable network shows. He is also the 1982-83 president of the New York Association of Cooking Teachers and sits on the standards committee for the International Association of Cooking Schools. An unqualified success, his school has bucked the notion that "you can't make a living by teaching cooking."

Most cooking teachers don't make their living solely by cooking, nevertheless. Rosemary Edesco has taught classes for 10 years, both in California and Colorado, mostly from her own kitchen and always part time. A wife and mother of three, she has resisted pressure to enter the profession full time and uses the profits from her school, Rosemary's Kitchen, strictly as a supplement to the family income. Rosemary reaps much of her reward from sharing what she knows with others who want to learn, and by making new friends with each new class.

ABOUT THE BUSINESS

Kinds of People You'll Teach

Cooking classes are taught to a wide variety of people, ranging from pre-teens to old age. Children are remarkably astute learners and will delight you with their creative flair. Senior citizens often enjoy instruction in quick and creative meal preparation, and they can be an especially appreciative group to work with. Young singles are usually well represented in cooking classes, partly because classes are fun and a good place to meet other like-minded singles.

Some classes are clearly aimed at working people, with special lunch hour sessions and weekend seminars arranged to focus on "quick cuisines." Other schools concentrate on advanced training for cooking professionals. This category includes such notable institutions as the California Culinary Academy, where chefs who plan to open their own restaurants are trained.

An unprecedented number of men are signing up for cooking classes these days. Some are doing it purely for practical reasons—such as recent divorces leaving them to fend for themselves. Others, however, are simply finding that cooking can be a relaxing and enjoyable hobby and an outlet for creative expression.

Eileen Albert, owner of Gourmet Gathering in Denver, reports that teaching men to cook can be a delightful experience. "The difference between men and women," she notes, "is that men have never been taught anything [about cooking]. They have primarily never had to cook, so the men that you get . . . are doing it because they want to. Besides, she said, they're often more creative "because they don't have any notions in their heads of what's 'right' and what's 'wrong.' They're free spirits."

Eileen believes that classes should be adjusted to meet men's tastes. They especially enjoy "heartier" meals, flambes, and other "showy" foods.

The type of students your school will attract will depend on the type of cuisine taught, your credentials and reputation, the fees you charge, and the type of learning atmosphere you're able to create. One of the most important factors is clearly the type of cuisine offered. Although Nouvelle and American cuisines are all the rage now on the two coasts, Judy Fauri of Panhandler Gourmet doubts that they will ever be popular in Denver: "People here just aren't interested in that kind of thing." According to Judy, the difference has to do with the lifestyle of the region, something you should consider before opening your own school.

After awhile, you'll begin getting return students and establish yourself with a specific type of clientele. It's this group to whom you should direct your major marketing efforts.

The Rewards of Teaching

Although owning your own cooking school may not make you rich, it could provide the perfect opportunity to become involved in more profitable food businesses. Many teachers simply won't give up their classes, even if they find financial success in another food area, because of the tremendous satisfaction they derive from sharing their love for cooking and the proper techniques and skills for foodcrafting. James Beard, Julia Child and Simone Beck are cases in point. Each are still teaching, far past the normal retirement age, and loving it.

In referring to the rewards of teaching, Rosemary Edesco said "It's a real kick! First of all, I meet all kinds of new people, they enjoy it, and I'm giving something to them. They really have a good time. It's a great ego thing for me to know that people come to my class, learn something, like it, say 'This is wonderful! I can't wait to come back,' and *do* come back. That's always very rewarding."

And the big plus, said Stan Levy, is that owning your own business offers a happy alternative to the corporate world of big bosses and little independence.

"The rewards," he said, "are that the business is your own; it's yours. You own everything. And, more than that, it's really a matter of how you spend your hours and what your day is like. It's much more comforting and rewarding, and a little bit less ulcer-inducing, than working for a large corporation. . . ."

If you love people, and you love teaching and cooking, the rewards for you as a cooking teacher will be great.

Profit Potential

It would be nice to be able to tell you that, by opening a cooking school and being frugal with your money, you could earn enough to retire in a few years. Because most people consider cooking classes an expendable luxury, however, they're reluctant to pay the kind of prices that can bring you a substantial profit. In addition, they usually don't recognize the expense and preparation that goes into making classes run smoothly and well.

Eileen Albert said, "I'm *constantly* developing recipes, doing them a second time to see what can be done ahead, and maybe a third time to see exactly how to teach it. . . ." She estimates that for each three-hour class she spends six to eight hours planning menus (because of her high number of repeat students she rarely repeats a meal), copying recipes for each student, shopping for ingredients, and cleaning up afterward.

Another profit-eater, she said, is the wear and tear on one's home. "There's a lot of potential for a mixer breaking or a lovely souffle dish smashing. So you have some extra expenses that, of course, people never anticipate." The advertising, food, equipment and rental bills, as well as the flowers or wine you buy for weekly after-class dinners, eat steadily into your profits.

Consequently, most cooking teachers rely on other sources of income for their primary support. Classes are taught as a way to meet interesting people, practice a favorite hobby, provide extra spending money or round out another type of foodcrafting business. Gourmet cookware and specialty take-out food shops often use schools as a draw for new business, but rarely make a substantial profit from their class operations.

There are, of course, notable exceptions. L'Academie Cordon Bleu in Paris has been the foremost center of the culinary world since 1895. Helen Worth's school, known as the "Radcliff" of cooking schools, had its first class in 1940. The reasons for these exceptions are obvious: world-famous names backed up by impeccable expertise. There is a certain snob appeal, of course, for taking classes at such schools.

Other schools, notably in "food-wise" cities where the income level can accommodate luxury, employ excellent local chefs and contract for exceptional guest lecturers. Others, backed by hefty investments and prudent managers, have survived the first few reputation-building years and now provide a tidy income for their owners. And some schools have been a catalyst for rising stars: Julie Dannenbaum, Anne Willan, Mary Risley, Charlotte Combe and others began by taking what they had learned from experts and then improved upon it in their own cooking schools.

The number of schools that provide primary incomes to their owners is, however, very small, and many find that teaching is best used as an inroad to other, more profitable foodcrafting businesses. Because cooking classes can be started on a shoestring and can lead to valuable contacts and reputations, they can be an ideal way to gain entry into many of the other foodcrafting businesses discussed in this book.

Training

Many of the teachers we interviewed have extensive training in their specialty area. Barbara Tropp, a popular teacher in San Francisco, spent 15 years learning Chinese cookery from Chinese families and spent two years in Taiwan. One teacher at Denver's Panhandler Gourmet has studied in six foreign countries, and others have apprenticed under accomplished and renowned chefs.

Credentials are important if you're planning to start a large school, and you should make sure yours are sufficient or else hire someone with the credentials you lack. But if you're only planning to teach pastry-making from your home kitchen, all you really need is a thorough knowledge of that specialty.

A background in teaching other subjects can be a real plus in a school of any size. The skills you've learned about demonstration, class management and presentations will transfer beautifully into the foodcrafting classroom.

Your Time Commitment

If you're looking for a job that will give you more time to spend with your family, a small school can be the answer. But think again if you're planning a full-scale operation: you'll probably spend 40 hours a week just mastering the various roles you'll have to play as a cooking school operator, including buyer, menu planner, bookkeeper, marketing expert, mail clerk and clean-up crew, to name a few.

At this point, a talent for time organization will play a vital role in helping you to keep your composure. If you don't have such a talent already, you're certain to develop one after you've operated your own cooking school for a year or two.

Having said all of that, there are also time advantages to opening your own cooking school because you, and not some distant corporate board, set the pace. You can start as small as you want, evaluate your time and money needs, and grow as slowly or as quickly as you like.

Advantages and Disadvantages of Size

Cooking schools run the gamut in size, from cozy home kitchen operations directed by cooks with talent but no credentials to hugh academies staffed with master chefs and attended each term by hundreds of students. If you're planning to teach, you've probably taken enough classes yourself to know that size can make a difference in how and what your students will learn. Small schools are sometimes criticized for their limited curricula, and large schools are criticized for being impersonal, inflexible or elitist. The truth is, there are good and bad schools of all sizes, and no particular size can claim superiority.

Although no specific size is inherently best, there are definite advantages and disadvantages to all sizes, and the size that's best for you will depend on the amount you can afford to invest, your credentials, and your plans for the school.

The minimal investment and the flexibility in determining operating hours which are typical of a small school are obvious advantages. Then too, small schools are usually very personalized and relaxed, and are usually much less expensive than their larger cousins. They may, however, lack the extensive range of cuisines and specialty techniques offered by larger schools.

Although larger schools are often staffed with expert chefs, they can be just as friendly as smaller schools, and as much fun. Anne Willan founded La Varenne in Paris to show that French cooking could be accessible and non-elitist, and has built an enviable reputation upon that premise.

Your Aspirations

As your school's popularity increases, you'll begin to think about adding extra classes or looking for new facilities to keep up with the increasing demand. Your decision on whether or not to expand will partly depend on your income and time requirements. If family hours are a priority and you don't need the extra money, you may choose to stick with teaching only two or three classes a week. But if your time is more flexible and your income requirements higher, your contacts from teaching can lead you naturally into catering, specialty foodcrafting, mail order, writing, or radio and television cooking shows.

Julia Child's famous *Mastering the Art of French Cooking* was the direct result of her experience as co-founder (with Simone Beck and Louisette Bertholle) of L'Ecole des Trois Gourmandes, their renowned French cooking school. Proclaimed a masterpiece, the book led to Julia's fame as an internationally requested lecturer and television cooking host. Julia's "The French Chef" was widely syndicated on educational television stations, and at the age of 70, she has a reputation as a world-acclaimed cooking authority that is undimmed.

Certainly Julia Child's experience is exceptional, but your expertise and commitment to quality can go far in turning your small cooking school into a thriving career.

REQUIREMENTS

Investment

One of the best things about opening a cooking school is that you can begin at any level you choose. Whether your budget is $100 or $100,000, if you have the know-how and the motivation, there's a place for you.

A small operation will do fine from your home kitchen, although you may need to purchase duplicate utensils and cookware. Advertising mailers or other promotion may take up the bulk of your budget in the beginning, but, all in all, you can open your school on a shoestring and gradually build it into a reasonably profitable and tremendously satisfying business.

Nancy Wiener created Nancy's Fancy in response to requests from friends that she teach them her culinary secrets. She invested in a new oven and a few utensils and began teaching from her California home, starting with the friends who had encouraged her in the beginning. She now teaches from eight to twelve students in each of her seven classes a year, and hopes to expand to one class a month. An established social worker, Nancy has no plans to build a full-time business but is using her classes to fund her own tuition for attending a cooking school in France. For Nancy, sharing her talent is a creative outlet that, happily, provides a welcome secondary income.

In contrast there is Ma Cuisine, a Los Angeles school whose chefs come straight from better-quality Los Angeles restaurants, complete with diplomas or established reputations, and whose students are often professionals brushing up on skills and techniques. Director Judy Gathers, a gourmet cook and author of several restaurant cookbooks, sees the business as a very serious venture whose aim is to teach students the mastery of a variety of cuisines. Five morning and four evening classes attract more than 100 students to each four-week term, at a total cost per person of $175-$225. There are five ovens and rangetops in the building, and enough utensils for each class of ten to twelve students. The success of the school—and it is financially successful—is attributable to its professionalism. According to Judy, the students "learn from some of the top chefs in the city," chefs who "teach as though they were dealing with professionals and not amateurs."

All of that costs money, of course, and Ma Cuisine did require a substantial initial investment. The investment paid off, however, with a school that has an impeccable reputation and a waiting list for many of its classes. Unlike most smaller schools, Ma Cuisine provides a primary income to its director, employs numerous part-time chefs, and makes a significant profit.

Equipment

Before you go out and buy two new rangetops and a double oven for the classes you're planning, consider this: most small operators use only their existing kitchen equipment to prepare class foods, although enrollment often reaches a dozen or more. The trick is to plan ahead. Pair or group classmates so that three dishes fill your oven instead of nine; cook as much as you can beforehand without affecting the quality of the meal or the integrity of the lesson; alternate mixing and cooking times between groups; share utensils and cookware. By doing this, you can be frugal with your initial investment and add utensils and cookware only as you need them.

Demonstration classes are noticeably easier to orchestrate than participation classes, requiring only a table that can be viewed by all classmembers, your existing equipment and plenty of chairs (which you can rent or borrow). You may also want to mount a mirror above your work table and angle it for increased visibility.

If your budget allows for new cookware, most teachers recommend going with name-brand, high quality products. Whipping your eggwhites in a copper bowl does make a difference, and your students will appreciate exposure to the best cookware and utensils you can afford. Any specialized cookware you need can be found at commercial restaurant supply houses, although prices are predictably high. Still, you can save money by comparison shopping and by bargaining when you buy in quantity.

Laws and Regulations

The laws and regulations covering the operation of your school will depend on its size, the kind of cooking you plan on doing, and your city and county zoning ordinances.

In many communities, schools with less than 50 or 75 students are considered to be "home industries" and are exempt from zoning regulations provided no traffic or parking problems are created. In other communities, no commercial cooking activities are allowed in residential areas, which means you'll have to spend money for rental space and possibly renovation and extra equipment costs. (Although some schools in such communities have operated for years on a "bootleg" basis out of residences, it is not recommended.)

If you don't plan to sell items you've cooked during class, your health department will probably have little to say about your school. They may want to give you advice on freezing, reheating and refrigerating food, but they are unlikely to inspect your kitchen unless they know you are selling food from it.

If you plan to branch into catering, mail order, or specialty foodcrafting, be certain to inform your health department prior to committing money to your plans. At least one cooking school was forced to put in new floors and walls, special sinks and drains, and make other expensive changes in order to comply with strict retail food codes when they added a catering sideline. Again, become informed of all relevant health department codes *before* committing any money to expansion plans.

Insurance

Although a cooking school is rarely considered a high-risk operation, you'll want to make some provision for general liability insurance coverage. It's unfortunate but true that having the public come into your home may well increase the chances of theft, so you may also want to add "contents" coverage to your homeowner's policy if you don't have it now.

Credentials

You don't necessarily need a fancy diploma or years of apprenticeship under a world-famous chef to run a successful cooking school. Many small schools are run by highly skilled cooks who simply didn't have the time or money to start out on a large scale. Though some frauds exist, most small operators are very knowledgeable about a particular ethnic, regional or national cuisine. They usually find that their students don't want or need a teacher with a Grand Diplome from Cordon Bleu, but only someone who can teach them the basics of the cuisines that interest them. These kinds of schools are fine for what they offer and usually provide a reasonable secondary income for their owners.

But if what you really want is name recognition, credentials are paramount. The world of cooking is, indeed, elite, and you'll find that diplomas from famous schools, acquaintances with famous authorities, thorough knowledge of particular cuisines, or the ability to hire people with those assets are your main hope of success in building a "name" school. In other words, your knowledge of your specialty must be extensive and complete, covering the most minute details and techniques. No one can make excuses for you if you try to teach students who know more about your subject than you or the teachers you hire.

Making a name for yourself, however, will come gradually and naturally if you continually strive for excellence. Generally, the more you know, the better your reputation and the higher the prices you can charge. Classes taught by such recognized experts as Julie Dannenbaum, Jacques Pepin or Anne Willan will always be filled, and James Beard, Julia Child and Simone Beck have been able to build culinary empires because of their extensive knowledge.

Business Sense

The larger your school is to be, the more specialized business knowledge will be required. A small school will require careful planning and organization, but only minimal bookkeeping and accounting. Larger schools, on the other hand, will require more extensive bookkeeping, the ability to negotiate and contract for services and supplies, and skills in public relations and general business administration.

When Judy Fauri and her partner opened Panhandler Gourmet, they were prepared to go for three years "without making a dime." "Most people who get into business are so poorly informed about what they're doing that they have challenges every time they turn around," Judy said. Because they had hired their legal and financial counsel, made financial arrangements with banks, and planned their business strategy well in advance of opening, their operation has been remarkabley crisis-free.

Your Teaching Abilities

Good cooks aren't always good teachers, but teaching skills, like cooking skills, can be learned, practiced, and eventually mastered.

One of the keys to effective teaching is organization. There are recipes to be decided upon, working spaces to be arranged, ingredients to be purchased, and lesson plans to be developed prior to every class. Without proper organization, cooking classes can be disastrous.

Good teachers are also friendly, helpful, well informed, very sociable, and able to communicate ideas and techniques easily and well. According to Judy Fauri of Denver's Panhandler Gourmet, "the classes that are most successful are taught by people who are creative, who have a flair and who are friendly. They're creative with food . . . and the finished product always looks very good." And, she adds, the best teachers "always have a lot of panache, or pizzazz."

You may be thinking that this sounds great for people who are naturally gregarious but that you have a problem with speaking before groups: namely that your knees tend to turn to jelly. Do yourself a favor and take a public speaking course prior to your first class session. You can learn to turn your nervousness into constructive energy and at least peacefully coexist with the butterflies in your stomach.

People Skills

The most popular teachers truly like other people and enjoy sharing their cooking expertise. Although he's one of America's foremost cooking authorities, James Beard still has time to offer friendly, helpful advice to students and others in the cooking business. Julia Child is famous for making people feel comfortable and welcome, even through a television screen. And in Denver, some students have studied with Eileen Albert for the entire ten years of her operation, a tribute to her school's family-like atmosphere and her ability to sense each individual's needs.

"I think a good cooking teacher has to work with the individual," she said. "You get a class like I do, and some of them have cooked a lot, some of them have not cooked very much, some of them are perfectionists, and some of them just care that it grossly turns out the way it should. So I think that you have to be able to really quickly assess the people in the class and work with them at their level, and bring them to where you want them to be."

This includes presenting information in a clear and precise manner and anticipating problems that students may face at home—things, she said, "that would never happen to you, but to a novice easily could. You really have to always be aware of the worst possible thing that could happen, and approach it that way."

According to Peter Kump, a good teacher must almost have a sixth sense about anticipating students' learning needs, but the most important thing is that they must build an atmosphere of complete, relaxed fun.

"I think it's very important that the teachers have a sense of fun," he said. "They not only should be knowledgeable, bright, and able, but should be able to coax the students and maintain an atmosphere that is a fun learning environment."

Eileen Albert clearly agrees that fun is important, and without it, she said, "you've defeated your purpose. If people don't enjoy it, if they don't see you enjoying it, they're not going to do it. It's just that simple."

THE NUTS AND BOLTS OF TEACHING

Starting Out

Now that you know something about cooking classes and the requirements for starting a cooking school, you must decide whether teaching is for you. Honestly consider the following questions:

• *Do you really love to cook?* Some people find that after teaching a few cooking courses, they'd really rather spend their working hours in a nine-to-five job, and reserve cooking for family meals, special occasions, or a pleasant way to spend free time. Your love of cooking must be a passion if you plan to make cooking a career. Nothing less will excite your students into enthusiastic effort.

• *Do you really enjoy people?* If you have trouble tolerating "silly" questions and the annoyances that can come from having a roomful of strangers come into your home, cooking classes may not be for you. Your love of people must be sincere; not only will you make a lot of friends because of it, you'll develop a reputation and a following.

• *Are you a good teacher?* Don't be fooled—leading a group of students in serious study while maintaining an enjoyable and pleasant atmosphere can be tricky. As Peter Kump says, "I think the most important thing in teaching is concern for the student. You know, are they learning or not? . . . I think if you're trying to get somebody to learn, that's the main thing." Quoting his friend Evelyn Wood, he said, "Just remember, if they haven't learned, you haven't taught."

• *Do you have a broad knowledge of your subject?* Although graduation from a top French cooking school is certainly not required, you should know enough about your material to qualify as a knowledgeable instructor. And, since you can never know it all, you'll probably need to keep taking classes yourself, and keep reading everything available about your specialty.

• *Is your business sense adequate?* You'll probably have to handle all your books and business communications yourself, at least at first. A course in accounting may be in order, and conversations with other cooking school operators can be helpful. (Those in your own community might be reluctant to share business secrets with a new competitor, but you'll probably find that cooking school operators in other cities are very open to "talking shop" with you.)

• *Can you survive on part-time pay?* It may take a few years to develop the reputation necessary to provide you a full-time income, so plan on finding some type of outside support until your finances are strong enough to handle the plunge into full-time operation.

If, after evaluating your answers to the foregoing, you still are interested in offering cooking classes, it's time to look into finding students.

Marketing Your Classes

Because of the small profit margins involved, most cooking schools can't afford extensive advertising and rely primarily on word-of-mouth to fill their classes instead.

A listing in the local yellow pages, together with inexpensive brochures or fliers distributed through cookware shops and posted on community bulletin boards may be all the promotion you need to get started. If you can obtain a mailing list from cookware shops or other likely sources you might also try a third-class bulk mailing to potential students. Eventually, of course, you'll develop your own list by keeping records of the people who have previously taken your classes and the names of friends they have recommended to you. Such a list can be invaluable assuming you've done a good job and your former students were fully satisfied with their class experience. You can then send simple course catalogs to this group several times each year, offering new cuisines and techniques as well as refresher courses on the basics of cooking.

You'll want to include enticing descriptions of your classes in such promotional literature, along with scheduled class times, prices, materials needed by class members, registration information, directions to your home or other location, and your phone number. Comments from satisfied former students, whether solicited or not, can also be helpful.

Larger schools advertise in local newspapers, and you may find it useful to list your school in the cooking school directories available in large newspapers. Remember that you'll need to repeat your ad for several months to get the best results.

As Peter Kump says, "If you find something that works, you need the repetition. We'll get calls from advertisements people have seen months before. Because it's there all the time, they'll remember it." And, he adds, the results are cumulative, drawing more response in the ad's tenth week than the third.

As a small school starting out, you should probably concentrate your marketing efforts on your local area. There is, however, a market for vacationers, especially if you live in or near a resort area, state or national park, or other popular destination. (If you're fortunate enough to live in such an area, ask you local Chamber of Commerce if they have any information on where most tourists visiting your area are from. Then investigate advertising and publicity opportunities in *those* areas.)

Publicity

When Judy Gathers invited food editors from the *Los Angeles Times* and *Bon Appetit* magazine to visit one of the classes at Ma Cuisine, they essentially provided all of the advertising she needed.

"If you invite some of those people to come in and watch some of the classes," she said, "they, in turn, spread the word" (if, indeed, they feel it's worthy of spreading). "And that's actually what happened with us," she said.

You can do the same for your school by inviting local food editors, television reporters or radio personnel to come by. Or send samples of your food along with brochures about your school to anyone in your local news media who can spread the word about your classes. Not all of them will choose to use the information you send, but even one good write-up could fill your classes for months.

You should use every opportunity to publicize your school, regardless of how small it is. Enter food fairs, bazaars, or local cooking contests. Many of your students will get a kick out of displaying the dishes they've learned to prepare in your class. You can offer free classes as prizes for contests, or enter them in auctions held for worthy causes. Encourage your students to give class gift certrificates to friends and family members. Tack some brochures and business cards to bulletin boards at supermarkets or laundries, and supply your library's community reference section with registration forms and brochures. Get to know the employees at local gourmet specialty and cookware shops; they often get questions about cooking schools and will probably refer people to the teachers they know best.

Scheduling Classes

One of the best parts of running a home school is that you can usually schedule classes around vacations, recreation plans and home activities. Your students will probably want to keep their holiday time free, which can be fortunate for you. (Many cooking teachers find that their pre-Christmas courses on special holiday foods fill weeks in advance, however.)

Cooking schools often follow an academic calendar (colder months invite indoor classes, especially baking classes), and courses in series can be conveniently split into fall, winter, spring and summer sessions. Determining the length of your sessions will depend on the variety of subjects you teach, your expertise in each, and the interest the courses generate. The more expert your knowledge, the longer your courses will generally be.

Before deciding which courses are best for you to teach, honestly assess your knowledge of each subject. Then, write out a complete course plan. Rehearse it with your family or friends to determine the best length for each class (and series of classes). Do you know a fair amount about a variety of special but unrelated dishes? Develop a number of one-day workshops, each covering a specific meal plan. Rosemary Edesco, a self-described "general cook," teaches a number of one-day classes, each targeting a different meal or food category. Or, perhaps your expertise covers all aspects of a particular cuisine. If so, multi-week courses and progressive sessions, like those of Peter Kump, will allow in-depth instruction, and the chance for you to see your class progress from the basics through the intricacies of haute cuisine.

You can tap specific markets by scheduling classes at unusual hours: what draws a blank on Tuesday night may be filled on Saturday morning. Lunch hour mini-classes are perfect for working folks; students and families will enjoy weekend seminars; and vacationers can plan well ahead for three- to seven-day intensive workshops. Finding the perfect schedule may take some experimenting; keep working at it until you've got the right combination to suit both you and your students.

Teaching Methods

You can teach your cooking classes by demonstration, student participation, or some mixture of the two. Experts say that demonstration classes are best for showing technique, but, as Judi Fauri says, "People love to play in mud. They love to participate." As your students copy your techniques, they will get a "feel" for the perfect consistency of creamy chocolate mousse, or the stacatto rhythm you use to chop onions. And you can squelch the development of bad habits by correcting poor technique as it occurs. But best of all, the atmosphere in a participation class is usually friendly and relaxed, as classmembers chat and work together to create something they can be proud of.

Still, most teachers contend students really learn more by watching the entire slicing, chopping, mixing, stirring and cooking process from beginning to end, and then practicing on their own.

The method that's best for you will depend on the type of dish or cuisine you're teaching, the kitchen space you have available, and the interests and skill level of the class. As you grow, experience will teach you which courses are best taught by participation or demonstration, or a particular combination of the two.

What to Include

Besides teaching a particular cuisine, some courses include

more general tips. Rosemary Edesco treats her students to a food shopping tour in Denver, where she points out fresh food markets, specialty cookware shops and her own favorite haunts. Most chefs will agree that presentation is a major part of gourmet meals, and many of them spend class time discussing artistic arrangements, color and texture combinations, and special effects. In fact, entire courses can be scheduled on food presentation alone.

Other areas you might cover include food drying, canning and freezing, bulk purchasing, and cooking for large groups. The key is to ask your students for ideas and feedback, and to try to fill any unmet needs you recognize.

Guest Lectures

Guest lectures are popular among students, and are a good way to introduce new students, or potential students, to your school. Unfortunately, the more familiar the name of your guest, the higher the price he or she can demand. And, according to one teacher, the prima donnas of the food industry can be nearly impossible to deal with.

"In most cases," Judi Fauri said, "it would cost thousands of dollars to have them here because, (a) they never fly anything but first class, (b) they never have just one staff person, they have to have their whole staff because they're generally not very well prepared, even though they would like to have you think they are, and (c), their cost of doing the class is also very expensive."

Not all cooking experts fit the above description of course, and some are delightful to work with. Still, the cost of bringing someone from San Francisco to Tulsa, for example, and providing accomodations, meals, and other expenses, can be totally out of reach unless you're absolutely sure that enough people will attend for you to at least break even.

A better bet for a small- or medium-sized operator is to begin with local and regional guests: a television or radio chef, newspaper food critic, or the owner of a popular catering company might be a good prospect. Capitalize, too, on friendships you've made through food-related associations and classes you've taken. Peter

Kump, through his natural warmth and genuine interest in people, long ago turned student-teacher relationships with James Beard, Simone Beck, Diana Kennedy and Marcella Hazan into solid friendships. He often delights his students by inviting his famous friends to guest lecture in his New York school or takes the students to them (most notably through his week-long classes in Simone Beck's French home).

When Things Don't Work

What happens when your cheese souffle falls flat and your upside-down cake refuses to leave the pan during the first meeting of your largest class? Well, says Eileen Albert, there's really only one choice. "You just laugh a lot, and you explain why it happened."

Surprisingly, Eileen says, people don't laugh at you, but with you. 'Actually, they love to see it. "They love to see you have a problem, because then they know that it's not going to be quite so awful if they have a problem at home."

Although slip-ups are embarrassing, they will happen to you, so expect them and be ready with a dash of humor. With humor, Eileen adds, "you can handle almost anything."

WHERE DO YOU GO FROM HERE?

Your established cooking school will probably attract numerous inquiries about catering, specialty foodcrafting, or other opportunities. Cooking schools are, in fact, an excellent way for you to enter a variety of other foodcrafting businesses. Mary Risley of Tante Marie's in Los Angeles was noticed by a local television station, and now she has her own cooking program. Barbara Tropp recently completed *The Modern Art of Chinese Cooking*, a 600-page book hailed as a masterpiece by critics. Other cooking teachers have written for magazines and newspapers, opened gourmet specialty or cookware shops, or used their income to enter completely unrelated fields. The extent to which your business can grow is really limited only by your imagination and your willingness to learn everything you can about cookery.

Gastronomic Tours

One business that deserves special mention at this point is gastronomic tour guiding. Once your cooking school is established and you've developed a good reputation in your community, organizing and leading food-oriented tour groups can be a pleasant extension of your teaching activities.

Picture this scene: somewhere in the green, rolling hills of France there is a small guest cottage with solid, whitewashed walls, a thatched roof, antique decor and robust, red-cheeked hosts. A crackling fire warms the sitting room and mounds of hearty, homecooked foods steam on the dining room table. A group of friends laugh and joke around the magnificent table, remembering the day's sightseeing trip to nearby towns and excitedly making plans for tomorrow's dinner—in one of Paris' famous three-star restaurants.

This scene is certainly appealing, and increasing numbers of people are willing to pay tour organizers to arrange tours which include such scenes, complete with ground transportation, accommodations, gourmet meals, an intimate atmosphere and common interests not usually found in other tour groups. Sparked by the increased interest in gourmet food and the rising availability of travel, people are looking for vacations that are far removed from the more commercial twenty-towns-in-twenty-days, eat-and-bolt tours, and innovative cooking teachers are answering the demand by arranging, marketing and leading trips that emphasize the kind of culinary samplings that delight gourmet food enthusiasts. If you have cherished memories of visits to France's intimate bistros (or even if you've never left your home state), you can cash in on the gastronomic tour business with a minimum of funds and, if you don't make an immense profit, at least you can finance your own vacation.

Where to Tour

Peter Kump was always looking for an excuse to return to France to visit his famous friend, Simone Beck. After she agreed to teach some of his friends, he organized a tour to her home outside of Nice, France. There he and eight students live for a week and study the art of preparing classic French cuisine, straight from one of the world's most recognized authorities. Cost: $1,870, not including air fare.

Stan Levy, owner of The Cook's Corner in Connecticut, was looking for a way to visit Italy and France without disrupting his business schedule and saw gastronomic tours as a perfect opportunity. Through a combination of local advertising, national publicity and the use of a 4,000-name mailing list, he organized tour participants and, in 1982, led his first gastronomic trip to France. Cost: about $2,000, excluding air transportation.

Giuliano Bugialli, the famous Italian cooking teacher, celebrates the opening of the local hunting season in the Umbria region of Italy with an eleven-day game feast and truffle-hunting expedition. Included in the $2,000-per-person cost (again, not including air fare) are visits to cultural landmarks, local festivals and vineyards, topped with four participation cooking classes in Bugialli's school in Florence.

Participants on other tours make the rounds of the restaurants of London, discover the secrets of making authentic Mexican hot sauces, and, wearing medieval costumes, feast in a Tyrolean castle. Picking a place for your tour can be as easy as picking a vacation spot you've wanted to visit. If you know of a beautiful place that's famous for food and has tourist attractions nearby, you have a potential destination for a gastronomic tour.

Most tour guides prefer to direct their attention to a region's major cities, where famous restaurants and historic landmarks keep the participants busy and well-fed. But there are also advantages to spending at least part of the tour in intimate, back-road inns, where tour members can sample the best of local foods and enjoy a part of the country that larger, more commercial tours rarely experience. If you're not familiar with a region's country inns, check with cooking teachers, chefs, or regional tourist bureaus for names and addresses, and then write each inn for brochures, information about their rates and accommodation limits, and a description of their facilities and the surrounding countryside.

How to Arrange Your Tour

When Peter Kump decided to revisit Europe with a group of students, he "wanted to show them the Europe I knew, the special places I remembered." He called a number of travel agencies and asked them to arrange a trip which would include sightseeing and lots of meals in Europe's finer two- and three-star restaurants. "Well," he said, " I found out then that they didn't even know what the good restaurants were! So I just made all the arrangements myself." That included arranging for transportation to and from airports, accommodations in "hotels with a little local color" as opposed to high-class (and high-priced) landmarks, visits to many of the kitchens in Europe's best restaurants, and, of course, a full schedule of gourmet meals across the continent. His familiarity with the region helped a great deal, and friends from the area helped with recommendations of their favorite restaurants and sights.

Before you begin arranging transportation and accommodations, you should know the exact number of tour participants you'll have. (Deposits from tour participants are essential, and you may wish to have a few alternates in case there are cancellations.) Most tours limit the number of participants to less than 25, and an average of ten to twelve works best for visits to smaller inns. You should contact other tours and travel agencies in your area to determine the best transportation deals, and read up on publications which will give you ideas about special events and sightseeing opportunities in the areas you plan to visit.

Most restaurants, hotels and airlines will require reservations for large groups, and may require a full or partial deposit. Timing is important, and your itenerary and reservations should be fully complete months in advance of your departure date. The process of planning, marketing, and arranging reservations for your tour may take you from six to twelve months.

One of the worst things that can happen on a tour is to arrive somewhere and discover that your hotel reservations or restaurant seats have been canceled or lost. Check and double check all reservations without fail. Get them in writing. Keep deposit receipts and have alternate plans in case everything else fails. The success of your tour (and your reputation as a tour leader) will largely depend on how smoothly things go and how you handle the unexpected situations that invariably occur.

Your Market

Why would someone want to pay $3,000 for a gourmet tour of France when they can go there independently for about half the price? "Why would a person want to hire a caterer when they can cook dinner for less?" counters Stan Levy. "They want to be pampered," he explains. "They want to be led; they want to be directed. They want an expert to tell them where to go. It's quality. There are all sorts of college groups and organizational groups that can tour for less, but not with the same quality, not the same restaurants, not the same places. And not the same style. It's not for everybody. . . . If it hurts to spend $3,000 for a gourmet tour, you shouldn't take it. It shouldn't put you in debt."

Although many of the tours include cooking instruction, he thinks most participants aren't looking for it. "They're not going there for an education. They're going for a vacation." It's important, therefore, for the tour guide not only to have a thorough understanding of the cuisine of the region but to be able to show the group places they would miss on conventional tours.

Because the market for gourmet touring is largely composed of high-income individuals, advertising should be focused on publications with high readership income levels. (You can request demographic information from targeted publications by writing their administrative offices.) Most prospective participants for this type of tour are between the ages of 30 and 60, with the median in the late 40s or early 50s, and almost all have at least a casual knowledge of gourmet foods (although there are some who go just for the fun of it.)

Peter Kump's five-day seminar at Simone Beck's French home filled up within weeks, but it can take months, or even a year to fill a specialized tour. The location of your school, your background as a tour guide and cooking teacher, your tour itinerary, and the income of your targeted market will play a large part in determining how quickly your tour will fill. "It's a marketing job," Stan Levy warned, and it takes imagination and perseverance to build a successful tour. To bolster your registration rate, contact food editors of major magazines and newspapers with your tour information, advertise in major metropolitan areas, and include information about your tour in your school's promotional mailings.

Your Profit Potential

Gastronomic tours are a good way to take a vacation. (But watch out, says Peter Kump. You'll find yourself "on stage" from 12 to 16 hours a day!) You probably will never get rich from organizing tours, however. Peter Kump makes about 10 percent profit on each tour; others probably make less. But, Stan Levy says, the chance to make regular visits to culinary capitals is worth it, and it just may bring you enough profit to make the trip worthwhile.

"The first time I went," he explained, "I said, 'All I want to do is put it together—not make money and get me a free trip.' And then when I looked at it a little closer I said, 'Well, I might as well get my wife and me a free trip,' and then I said, 'Well, I can maybe make a little money out of it." Has he? "I don't know," he said laughing. "I'll tell you in five years."

Whether or not you make a profit from your first trip, there are certain tax advantages to running a gourmet tour when you have another food-related business. Ask your accountant for details on the deductions you can expect to take.

Chapter 6
Take-out Shops and
Gourmet Food Shops

Have you ever wanted to open your own shop? Ever-increasing demand for gourmet-quality food is creating unique opportunities for would-be shopkeepers, and selecting the right products and decor for a quaint shop in the perfect location—and watching it become successful—can be tremendously satisfying.

Take Out Shops

In 1977 Sheila Lukins and Julee Rosso began cooking some very special foods, including pickled wild cherries, blueberry chutney, venison stew, spinach pate, blackberry mousse, soups, nutcakes, breads, and cookies. Each day the aroma of these delightful foods, among others, filled a tiny 11 × 16 storefront on Manhattan's West Side and spilled into the streets, confronting passers-by with a relentless call to sample and savor. Unable to resist the aromatic temptation, pedestrians did, indeed, file in, and soon a horde of customers were clamoring for more of Julee and Sheila's creative cooking.

The two women were no strangers to pleasing people. Previously the advertising director for Burlington Industries, Julee already knew how to sell an idea. Sheila was a housewife in late 1976 when Julee hired her to cook a press breakfast for one of her accounts. The outstanding fare left an impression with Julee, and, when she left Burlington a month later and decided to open a take-out shop as a hobby, she gave Sheila a call. Over the next few weeks the scheme for a part-time venture blossomed into a full-time commitment for a combination catering and take-out business.

Julie and Sheila pooled their mutual savings of $21,000. With it, they rented a tiny storefront (still in use today) and filled it with cloth-lined bread baskets, beribboned cinnamon sticks, old-fashioned cookie jars packed to the brim with four varieties of chocolate chip cookies, calico-covered jars of fruits, marmalades, chutneys and preserves, and dozens of other delicacies, all surrounded by cool, white tile, gleaming brass, butcher-block counters and clear, sparkling glass.

In the jam-packed little room, Sheila did the cooking and Julee handled sales, catering prospects, and logistics, mostly from a stool near a less-cluttered wall. Local businesses sent "emissaries" to try the new foods, hoping for relief from the monotony of standard deli fare. What they found, according to one New York magazine reporter, was a business with a "silver palate," a name that Julee and Sheila adopted to emphasize the high quality of ingredients used in their products. After two months the two entrepreneurs were keeping up with bills and paying off their investment, and soon they were looking for a new kitchen, contracting with canning and packaging companies, hiring new chefs, and facing the growing pains typical of rapidly expanding businesses. They quickly found they needed to split their own duties and hire others to handle things like store management, sales, typesetting, and public relations, leaving the two women free to develop marketing plans and work on improving and expanding their lines of gourmet foods. By 1983 the Silver Palate had 30 employees, including a five-member national sales team, a catering coordinator, a head chef, and a public relations expert.

The growth of Julee and Sheila's staff reflects the growth of their business. From the small, original storefront they've grown to the point where they supply nearly 700 retail shops across the nation. Their catering business services both small households and hugh corporations. A new mail-order catalog went to 45,000 homes across the U.S. in December, 1982, and *The Silver Palate Cookbook*, co-authored by the two women, has sold well over 150,000 copies in its first five printings.

The Silver Palate is a tremendous success for its owners, who are both sharp businesswomen and excellent cooks dedicated to impeccable quality. And, according to Julee, they've only begun to explore the possibilities of success with their foods.

Julee Rosso and Sheila Lukins have built one of the nation's most respected gourmet food businesses by creating a consistant supply of top-notch specialty foods. But you can do well with just one great item, or a combination of a few very special ones.

Gail and Roy Cohn and John Heuer are partners in the Bonnie and Clyde Ice Cream Parlour, a small take-out store near the Santa Monica beach. Featuring ice cream, chocolate chip cookies, brownies, and fresh, flavored popcorn, the shop is a sweet spot of memorabilia and fantasy. Walls, popcorn tins, paper products, and assorted packages are illustrated with pictures of the famous outlaw couple, and a caricatured model of Bonnie and Clyde's getaway car stands in place of a counter, the long, low midsection filled with goodies. A machine that pops up 22 flavors of popcorn, including pineapple, licorice, coconut, and caramel chugs along inside the passenger section of the car. The snacks served in the parlour are clearly a hit, and by 1983 the business had expanded to include wholesaling and mail-order departments and six other shops across the country were patterned after the original Bonnie and Clyde Ice Cream Parlour theme.

Laura Katleman and George Montilio opened a take-out shop in Boston with only one product—brownies. Inexperienced at 22, Laura had a difficult time finding a building that would rent even the smallest space to her, but after a year she convinced one landlord that her idea was worthwhile. Investing $1,000 each,

Laura and George opened shop. With 20 varieties of specialty brownies and a special Brownie-Gram (one and a half pounds of pure chocolate goodness, topped with a message of up to ten words), Boston Brownies grossed $500,000 in the first year, and 20 percent of that was profit.

In Aspen, Colorado, cookieholics flock to the opening doors of Chip Chip Hooray, a bakery that cooks one of the world's favorite sweets—chocolate chip cookies. In other cities, customers line up for pizza-by-the-slice, Middle Eastern falafels (meat and vegetable combinations stuffed into pita bread) and other ethnic treats, desserts, snacks, candies, and a wide range of specialty foods. And some take-out shops, like Georgetown's famous Pasta, Inc., feature complete meals-to-go, from the appetizer to after-dinner wine.

As two-income families become the norm and households shrink in size, people increasingly look to carry-out food to fill their needs. Busy executives like quick take-out meals, young people can rarely resist indulging in snacks, elderly folks appreciate the convenience of ready-made salads, entrees, and desserts, and noontime crowds will do practically anything to avoid the monotony of brown-bag lunches. From coast to coast, take-out sales are brisk. If this type of business appeals to you, the first thing you need to consider is your market.

Market Study

One of the most important tools in shaping your retail path to success is the market study. Through it, you can determine how well your product fits the needs and wants of a given population or a segment of a given population and where to set up shop to most effectively tap that market. Even if you can't afford a professional study, you can effectively determine the success potential of your take-out venture by carefully considering these factors:

 • *Your Product.* Is it really unique? Old and new favorites, like cookies, brownies, croissants, and chocolates are good sellers, but only if they're better than the products people can find in a supermarket or convenience store. Your insistence on using only the finest ingredients will make believers out of first-time customers. But don't just guess about taste—test it! Visit luncheon clubs, auctions, social clubs, sororities, friends, relatives, anyone who will give you an honest opinion of your specialty. You may wish to hand out a short questionnaire with each sample (one that can be filled out while your product is still melting in the person's mouth) asking for ratings on freshness, taste, and qualities such as moistness, flakiness, firmness, and so forth. Then question each taster: Would you buy this in a retail store? Does your supermarket carry anything similar? Where would you most like to see this product? How often would you buy it? How much would you pay?

Polly Daly, owner of Chip Chip Hooray, tested batch after batch of chocolate chip cookies on friends and acquaintances, adjusting the recipe each time until, at last, she found a cookie that was delicious and would remain soft and moist even in Colorado's dry climate and high altitude. Polly's friends warned her against opening a retail outlet for the cookies. A tight economy and the problems of retailing had seen many shops fail in Aspen. But armed with her market tests, Polly opened anyway, and her studies paid off. Tight money notwithstanding, the cookies were a hit and have developed such a following that cookie addicts line up outside the shop, waiting for the doors to open. One of the reasons Polly had such success was because she adjusted her recipes after thoroughly testing them—a practice you would do well to follow.

If your take-out shop is to sell an entire line of foods, testing becomes more complicated. Pick the products you think will have the broadest appeal. Test main entrees, desserts, and snack items first, leaving side dishes, condiments, and beverages for later testing in the store. Most take-out shops rely on a half dozen or so very special products for most of their business. These are the products that people identify with the shop's name. Other products come and go with demand.

Always keep an eye out for new recipes, and give even the most unlikely ones a trial run. Many shop owners have been surprised at the unusual items that suddenly catch on. Spinach-filled croissants, deep fried ice cream, chocolate covered pretzels, vegetarian casseroles, and whole wheat pasta are just some of the foods that, overnight, seemed to capture the tastebuds and imaginations of American consumers. Full-line shops have a virtually endless choice of new items to test. Selecting the perfect ones may just be a matter of trying out a wide range of high-quality foods on your local market. For one-product shops, the perfect food may be a variation on an old recipe. Some of the brownies at Boston Brownies, for example, are made with imported liqueurs—a unique feature that has proved to be extremely popular.

• *Your Market.* The age, educational level, income, culinary sophistication and lifestyle of your market will have a variety of effects on your operation. The location you choose, your shop's interior decor, the slant of your advertising, and the prices you charge should reflect the characteristics of that segment of the population which most often buys your food (your market, in other words). To get a good understanding of the demographics of your market, choose different test spots, carefully noting the appearance of the neighborhood, apparent affluence of people tested, their approximate age and their interest in your product. Professional studies often include extensive questions about such matters, but your pointed observations may do the job just as well.

• *Your location.* A smart businessperson would never dream of opening a charcuterie in an area surrounded by tract houses and low-income households, yet every year thousands of retailers close their doors for good because they misjudged the importance of location. Some of the important factors to consider in choosing your location are population density, foot and street traffic levels, nearby competition, the economic characteristics of the area, developments in the area (will there be heavy construction obstructing traffic from your door?), and whether the neighborhood is a business, residential, suburban, or mall area. Nadine Kalichnikoff, owner of Pasta, Inc., picked the perfect spot for retailing her handmade pasta dishes and full-course meals. The posh Georgetown store draws lots of affluent customers from the thousands of passers-by, and in the first six weeks of business, Nadine's sales totaled $75,000—a testimony to the importance of carefully choosing a location.

Once you've narrowed your choices to a few locations, visit each one, taking notes on specific neighborhood characteristics. The importance of pedestrian traffic can't be emphasized enough, and it's a good idea to count the people walking by each potential site so you'll have a good basis for comparison. If you're considering a mall location, is your site in the main thoroughfare, or in one of the crannies that people tend to pass by? A few extra footsteps may make the difference in whether shoppers notice your store or hurry by, empty-handed. If located on a busy street, does your proposed site have ample parking? Is it easily visible from the street? Outdoor malls (especially the ones with cobblestone streets and quaint little shops) offer an almost guaranteed market, yet rent is often exorbitantly high, so sales must be doubly good to meet overhead costs. Upstairs and basement shops don't draw nearly the crowds that ground level stores do, and stores only a block away from the main shops may get only a fraction of the business that their better-located neighbors get.

The condition of the building is another important consideration in choosing the location of your take-out shop. Will extensive remodeling be needed? Are there features that must be repaired, replaced, or rebuilt in the near future? What about plumbing, electricity, heating, and air conditioning? Are they adequate? Energy efficient? Building maintenance costs can quickly add up, so be certain that the space you choose needs only minimal work or that you have plenty of capital to cover changes down the road.

If you plan to cook in the same building from which you retail, be sure the area zoning will permit it. Check with health department officials and zoning departments before signing any lease. Remember that you'll be paying a premium price for cooking in a retail building, and you may be better off renting or remodeling a kitchen in a less expensive industrial or warehouse area and transporting your foods to the retail store. Some businesses, such as cookie shops in malls, have their foods mixed in a separate kitchen but do the baking in the storefront, where the aroma drifts out and draws customers in that might otherwise pass by.

The Basics of Starting a Take-out Business

If a take-out business sounds like a natural for your product or food line and a market study confirms your ideas, you need to consider a number of details involved in take-out shop operations. Because some of the production steps are the same as those in specialty foodcrafting businesses and the marketing procedures are the same as with gourmet specialty shops, you may want to review those chapters in this book. Here, we'll briefly talk about finding a kitchen and the right equipment, the legal considerations involved in take-out businesses, pricing, advertising, interior design, and your possibilities for expansion.

Decorating the Interior

The inside of your shop can have as much of an effect on sales as the quality of your food. Restaurants sometimes pay interior design companies hundreds of thousands of dollars to create the perfect atmosphere for them, and although you needn't invest your entire savings into it, you too should pay careful attention to design. Roy and Gail Cohn attracted attention to their Bonnie & Clyde Ice Cream Parlor with their getaway car-turned-counter; Sheila Lukins and Julee Rosso added special charm to The Silver Palate with their creative attention to detail, using ribbons, bows, calico, and old-fashioned wicker baskets to accent their delectable products. Pasta, Inc., is the perfect picture of sparkling cleanliness, with white walls, smooth, white ceramic tiles, white ceiling fans, and gleaming metal racks. Decorating every spare corner are fresh, bright flowers, and dried herbs hang from a skylight over the front counter.

Designing a take-out shop can be fun, but if you lack the talent for interior design you may do well to hire a professional. A good firm will help you fit the best possible decor to your budget, a factor that will go a long way in building your store's image and atmosphere.

In the Kitchen

Although many take-out shops have kitchens right in the storefront, you may want to rent or remodel a kitchen in another, less expensive area.

Remodeling can be tremendously expensive. While existing kitchens can often get by with older equipment and outdated features, new ones must comply with the most recent laws and regulations, often involving special plumbing, heating, air conditioning, equipment, and furnishings. You may find that renting a kitchen is much more feasible. If so, consider renting from resorts, churches, restaurants, bakeries, wholesale food manufacturers, caterers, or civic groups. Many of these have kitchens that are in use only part of the day, and will probably rent their space and equipment to you at a reasonable rate. Remember to check with health officials before moving in, since a kitchen that is approved for sandwich making, for example, may not meet the requirements for more involved foodcrafting.

Equipment

Second-hand equipment is, of course, much less expensive to buy than new equipment. A good restaurant supplier can provide you with high quality used equipment, or you may be able to share equipment used in the kitchen you rent. Other sources for equipment and cookware bargains include auctions, liquidation sales, and surplus stores and sales.

Some companies lease new equipment, including ice machines, refrigerators, ovens, and other large items. Check terms, making sure that repairs are paid by the rental company and that, at the end of the term, you have the option to buy the old equipment or lease newer equipment. For more information on finding a kitchen and the right equipment, refer to the Specialty Foodcrafting chapter in this book.

Your Price

Some products fail because people simply aren't willing to pay their high price, although they may be excellent products otherwise. A good market study will pinpoint the upper limits of the price you can reasonably charge your customers. In the meantime, consider the prices of competitive products found in supermarkets, convenience stores, and fast food shops. Because you are a new business, your prices will probably be higher. In the mind of the customer, does the quality of your product justify the higher price?

To determine the optimum price to charge for a product, make a full batch of it, keeping an exact account of all ingredients used and their prices. Even spices and other ingredients used in small quantities should be considered in your figures. A teaspoon here and a tablespoon there don't cost much at first, but the pennies will quickly add up when you produce bulk quantities of your product. You'll also need to calculate the cost of wastage. Vegetables, salads, and other fresh foods have an extremely short shelf life, and you may find yourself throwing a lot of them away at first. If your budget doesn't cover it, profits can quickly be affected. Finally, include the cost of labor and overhead in your expenses, and then add an appropriate profit margin.

Legal Considerations

Where you live and the type of shop you operate will determine which laws cover the operation of your take-out business. An in-store kitchen may require you to meet the same codes that affect stand-up restaurants, whereas shops which bring in food from commissary kitchens are treated more like other retail food outlets. To determine which laws cover your particular take-out venture, contact your local licensing authorities, as well as local zoning, fire, and health departments. A great deal of planning, negotiating, adjusting, and patience are often required in dealing with these government bodies. For help, talk to other retail shop or restaurant owners; their experience with local authorities can be helpful as you try to comply with the various departments and regulations covering your business.

Advertising

Until you get to the point where word-of-mouth referrals and repeat business carry you along, you'll probably need to use some form of advertising. See the section on advertising in the Specialty Foodcrafting chapter of this book for ideas.

New Horizons

Sheila Lukins and Julee Rosso built a multimillion dollar business from a tiny retail store by expanding into several other food areas, including wholesaling, mail order, and cookbook writing. Gail and Roy Cohn have done the same with their popcorn, packing flavored varieties in decorated tins to be shipped to other retailers and mail-order customers across the country. You can diversify with your foods, too, once your business is well established and you can afford the commitment it takes to expand into other areas. Food fairs are a good place to meet other retailers who might be interested in selling your product in their stores, and your own customers may provide you with names of friends and relatives around the country who may enjoy ordering from a mail-order brochure. To find out more about the details of such businesses, review the appropriate chapters in this book.

Running a take-out store can be fun and rewarding. Cooks almost universally talk about the pleasure that comes from sharing a special recipe with others. If you can make a good living by doing just that, how much the better!

Remember though, that opening and running a take-out shop can be both expensive and time consuming. The hours are long, and investment requirements can be high. But if you think you have the commitment necessary to see it through, access to the investment capital needed, and a product that's a winner, the take-out business may be right for you.

GOURMET FOOD SHOPS

Gourmet and specialty food shops are riding the crest of the specialty food wave, with offerings of every imaginable food to their 10 million customers. At a time when traditional grocery stores are reporting annual sales gains of 9 percent, gourmet shops report gains of a whopping 20 percent and are pulling in half again as many profits as their traditional counterparts, a fact that has supermarket giants hopping in their boots to find ways of keeping up.

One of the most successful specialty markets in America is Dean & Deluca, the brainchild of two New York City entrepreneurs who, in 1977, invested $150,000 in their gourmet food import venture and parlayed it into a 1982 sales figure of $8 million. Beginning with a small line of imported gourmet items which they sold from a SoHo retail store, Dean & Deluca now wholesale their line of almost 100 products to over 800 retail outlets across the country, as well as stocking their own popular shop. The Dean & Deluca name stands for such high quality and high standards that it is a household word both in the industry and among consumers, and each year people stand in line at food fairs to see their newest imported products.

All over the country, similar shops are experiencing comparable growth. Consumers are eager to taste new and exotic foods and have all but given up on finding them in supermarkets. The success of gourmet food shops is at least partly attributable to their upscale clientele who, according to one owner, "will always have the money to buy whatever they want." Not everyone who appreciates gourmet food fits this discription, of course, and many gourmet shop customers manage to eat very well on limited budgets. Willing to scrimp on vacations and entertainment, these people nevertheless allow themselves to splurge on good food. As Stacey Bremers, co-owner of Essential Ingredients in Boulder, Colorado, says, "I think that instead of going to a restaurant and dropping $200 to have fresh Beluga caviar and Dom Perignon served to them, people would just as soon buy the ingredients, make it at home and spend only $50."

One of the interesting points about gourmet specialty shops is that they seem to have a self-perpetuating clientele. While increased interest in gourmet items created a need for specialty shops, the expanding variety of foods to be found on their shelves increasingly tempt shoppers, who discover new favorites and soon get into the habit of visiting their favorite gourmet shop on a regular basis. And, because gourmet shops often have a friendlier, more personalized atmosphere than is found in supermarkets, as well as greater attention to service, shoppers almost invariably prefer gourmet shops.

Start-up Requirements

Whereas most other gourmet and specialty food businesses can be started with minimal investments, gourmet specialty shops depend on fairly large inventories and attractive retail space to build a clientele. Stacey and Robert Bremers spent $40,000 in 1979 to buy 1,000 gourmet foods for Essential Ingredients, but warn that they wouldn't do it again with less than 2,500 products and an initial investment of $250,000. For the first year the Bremers struggled along, borrowing money from their parents when they ran short and hoping that their dream would pay off. It did, but not before they faced several financial crunches. "We were really lucky," Stacey said. "We both had parents who could finance us. If it weren't for them, we would have gone under many times."

Winning Characteristics

Aside from having adequate investment capital, a successful

gourmet food shop owner must be a jack-of-all-trades. As you set up and run your retail store you'll have to play the roles of purchaser, food expert, inventory clerk, marketing specialist, janitor, and social whiz, among others. And, as in any retail business, a hefty dose of patience and a genuine love of people is essential. With those qualities, the day-to-day dealings with customers, wholesalers, bankers, suppliers and partners are transformed from a headache to a fulfilling way of life. By paying special attention to the needs and personal lives of their customers, the Bremers have not only made friends, but built a broad customer base of those who regularly visit their store. "People sort of like the ma and pa atmosphere here," Stacey said. "I think it really gives them a very comfortable sort of feeling to know that we're here and that we're interested. . . . I think that really makes a difference."

Product Knowledge

Because good service is such an important part of running a successful gourmet food shop, customers will come to expect (and appreciate) your guidance and suggestions on food storage, preparation, and serving. With hundreds of eager wholesalers presenting new products each year, it can be quite a job just to keep up with what is available. To do so, you must read food magazines, visit food fairs, and search out other gourmet specialty shops for items you may not know about. The Bremers opened their store with just the foods Stacey knew about from her own gourmet cooking, but with the aid of a suggestion box in the store, soon came up with 3,000 of the most popular items for their market. Stacey warned that there are "in" foods every year: one year, it was raspberry vinegar, another year, pink peppercorn. Because there is so much media coverage of such novelties, customers are sure to request them and ask about their use, so you'll need to be prepared with suggestions gleaned from food fairs, trade journals, food manufacturers, and your own experimentation.

It's important to note that perishables take a lot more effort to retail than canned or boxed foods. As Stacey said, "Fresh fruits and meats take a lot of know-how. . . . You just really have to know

what you're doing to make it work.'' Be sure to check with the
health department before you buy any perishables, and learn
everything you can about refrigeration requirements and shelf life.
For information, contact your health department or local meat and
dairy council.

Choosing a Location

The success of your gourmet food shop will depend to a very
large extent on your location. Unlike supermarkets, specialty food
stores attract much of their business from passers-by and impulse
shoppers, and few customers are willing to travel across town on
weekly shopping trips for gourmet items. Before you sign a store
lease, thoroughly consider the location and ask yourself these questions:

• *What is the neighborhood like?* Are families large or
small? Do they live in single- or multi-family units? What is
the general standard of living? What other businesses exist?
Do they appear to have affluent customers? What are the
needs and wants of the community? While suburban families
may enjoy an occasional gourmet dinner, their habits may
run more toward fast food outings, and low-income areas can
rarely afford to test new specialty foods. Frost & Sullivan,
market analysts for the food industry, report that typical
gourmet customers are between the ages of 25 and 44 and
have a household income of over $30,000. They come from
small household units and care about quality, status, and the
healthfulness of food products. To make sure your gourmet
shop targets the right market, locate your shop in close prox-
imity to large numbers of these types of people.

• *What is the competition?* If the supermarket down the
block offers the same items, you're out of business. What
about fresh fruit markets, farmers' markets, and other
gourmet shops in the area? If you're going to develop your
own clientele, be sure to offer a variety of foods that differ

from those normally available to consumers in the neighborhood.

• *How heavy is pedestrian traffic?* Downtown business districts with their large concentrations of executives and white-collar workers on lunchbreaks, as well as shoppers and sightseers can be perfect for gourmet shops. Outdoor malls are also good, but rent can be exorbitant. If your site has little or no pedestrian traffic, be sure that ample parking space is available, preferably at no cost to the customer, and that your store is easily visible from a major street.

Other considerations include the amount of usable space available and the condition and appearance of the building. Be sure that you have ample space for expansion and plenty of room to store excess inventory. Remodeling may be expensive if you have to install major equipment to meet strict health code standards. Check with health and zoning departments for the requirements in your area.

Before You Begin

Getting ready to open a retail food business involves plenty of hard work selecting inventory, arranging sources of supply from food wholesalers, hiring employees, establishing accounting and inventory systems, advertising, and determining prices. Most of this depends on your own good instincts about what will work, but you can increase your business acumen by talking to other retailers and reading any of a number of good books and articles written about retail businesses. (See Appendix A.)

Expanding

Helen and Dick Allen of San Francisco's Wine and Cheese Center have set up tasting rooms where customers sample delicious cheeses and learn about compatible wines (from a staff member or from one of the Allen's new computers) before making their purchases. The Oakville Grocery, also in San Francisco, draws new customers every time celebrity cooks use the store and its ingredients in cooking demonstrations. Fully one-third of Dean & Deluca's annual sales come from its newly founded wholesaling business, and the Bremers, who own Essential Ingredients, have added a kitchen to their small retail outlet and cook fine pastries and full meals for customers on the go. Expanding in the gourmet food business can be easy, and just about any idea may work once you've got your own retail outlet and established clientele. Consider packing picnic baskets, or cater elegant breakfasts in bed. Catering to private parties or business conventions can be a profitable sideline, and you may want to start your own wholesaling branch from the recipes you try.

Chapter 7
Other Foodcrafting Opportunities

One of the nice things about foodcrafting is that there are as many opportunities as there are creative ideas. By taking a look at the world of food and the needs and wants of American consumers, you may come up with your own unique business idea. This chapter provides a sampler of ideas that have worked for others.

ONE PERSON'S EXPERIENCE

In 1980 Clarence Jolley set up a system for delivering baskets of gourmet foods and beverages to food lovers anywhere in the continental United States. Modeled after the monumentally successful Florists' Transworld Delivery system, Dial-A-Gift now reaches more than 1,200 retail outlets—mostly fancy food stores and liquor shops in Canada, Mexico, France, England, and parts of the Caribbean, as well as all 50 states.

Dial-A-Gift is the outgrowth of a similar system called Telecake, also created by Jolley, which delivers decorated cakes through 3,000 retail bakeries. Jolley sold that business when he found the demand for gourmet foods outstipping that for cakes. "People were always asking, 'Can I order cheese? Can I order fruit baskets . . . ?' So we created Dial-A-Gift in answer to that."

Gift orders are taken via a toll-free telephone number, and customers choose from baskets of cheeses, fresh fruits, steaks, candies, gourmet foods, dried fruits and nuts, wines and champagnes. Then, a general price range is discussed, and sometimes a customer will request a certain brand name or label. Special occasion and holiday baskets can be ordered, like the popular Love Basket for Valentine's Day. Get-well packages are popular for the hospitalized. The gifts are made to order at the local retail outlet, and deliveries are made in 24 hours or less in most areas, with 48-hour delivery guaranteed.

Clarence started Dial-A-Gift on a medium-sized shoestring, visiting gourmet shops and liquor stores all over the country in person, but sleeping in his car to save money. Today, revenues for sales top $1 million annually, and "we're still growing" Clarence says. In fact, it's gotten so popular that gourmet food shops are waiting in line to be included in the program, and "some of the biggies are trying to buy us out!"

Dial-A-Gift is really a one-of-a-kind national business, but it shows that by recognizing a need you can build a satisfying and unique business and supply the public with something it wants. Hundreds of others are doing the same. A catering service in New York specializes in delivering luxurious breakfasts in bed, and another in Los Angeles prepares full meals for bachelors and others who hate the thought of cooking daily meals. Many cookware companies hire professionals to demonstrate their wares by preparing full meals at conventions, in cookware stores, and at cooking seminars. What you want to do is up to you, and with enough effort you can do just about anything in the world of cooking and turn your love of food into profits.

THE FREELANCE CHEF

An exciting new category of foodcrafting is gaining popularity. While party hosts enjoy the luxury of entertaining guests without the responsibility of cooking, a freelance chef creatively works in the kitchen, whipping up a meal to please the most discriminating palates. Unlike a caterer, however, a freelance chef does everything from the home of the host, using fresh ingredients to concoct fabulous meals from scratch.

John Fifield, owner of Rent-A-Chef in Denver, thinks food prepared on location is far superior to food cooked in a commissary kitchen. "There is just no way you can prepare food, haul it in a truck, and then try to serve it and have it as tasty and as fresh as if you do it on location," he insists.

John, who had been "behind the swinging doors" for 15 years before opening his own freelance cooking outfit, got the idea for the business after a trip to Europe, where chefs hire themselves out for a day, a week, or a year to those who don't have their own live-in cooks. The idea has worked equally well in Denver. John has served candlelit dinners for two, banquets for 2,000, and everything in between.

A booking goes something like this: a client calls up with a request for John's services. John asks them to describe the occasion they have in mind. Next, they discuss specifics: What is the atmosphere to be? How is the meal to be served? What kind of china is preferred? Are there food preferences for the event? Then, visiting the kitchen, John surveys the equipment and cookware, noting those things he'll have to provide himself. Those items are rented from a local kitchen and restaurant supplier, with the fee charged to the client. Bartenders, waitresses and waiters, and cooks' assistants are scheduled from a list of part-time, temporary help. A deposit of $1 per guest is paid in advance, the remainder on the date of the event. Food is purchased from a wholesale supplier or fresh food market, usually only a few hours before the event is scheduled to begin. Often, cooking requires two trips to the kitchen—once to pop meats and long-cooking items into the oven, and again just before the event to actually prepare the meal.

In addition to complete meals, Rent-A-Chef offers "The Executive Service," an opportunity for working women—and men—to serve a meal of maximum taste with minimal hassle. Contacting the Rent-A-Chef firm, the client will choose from five available menus. Then, leaving a key for the arriving chef, the client can leave for work knowing that one of John's four trained chefs will take full responsibility for preparing the evening meal. Arriving home, the client finds the table set, pots and pans full of delicious foods, and instructions for heating and serving the meal.

Besides executives, John often serves single parents, conventions, couples, and folks who are "just plain tired" of eating out in restaurants. Prices are about the same as for catered meals, running from under $10 a person for informal gatherings to $20 or $30 for formal sit-down dinners.

One of the advantages of becoming a freelance chef is that it costs even less to enter than catering. John Fifield started out with a "hat, an apron, and a $50 ad." Because the kitchen is provided by the client, potentially exorbitant kitchen rental fees are avoided. It can be started part-time and expanded smoothly into a full-time career. And, long-term contracts (some of John's contracts run a year or more) are valuable for providing a good financial base from which to expand.

Still, as John said, "like with any other small business, you take your chances" being a freelance chef. To optimize your chances of success, thoroughly consider the needs and wants of your community. Is the population base large enough to provide a full-time career as a freelance chef? What is the relative sophistication of people in your community? Will they pay for quality foods? Next, assess your cooking skills, organizational skills, and commitment. Can you sell your service? Can you follow up a good sales pitch with excellent service?

If you are a creative and talented cook and want a low risk way to make your skills pay off, freelance cheffing could be for you.

PUSHCART VENDING

Like a picture out of the past, a brightly colored popcorn wagon stands on a pedestrian mall corner in downtown Aspen,

Colorado. With its old-fashioned clapboard siding, antique letter- ing and the enticing smell of freshly popped, buttery corn, it draws smiles and plenty of business from those passing by.

Although pushcart venders have been around for decades in some cities, they have made a big comeback in the last few years and, following closely on the success of pedestrian malls, they're ringing up impressive profits on such items as hot dogs, peanuts, Mexican foods, Italian "ices," and dozens of other low-cost foods.

In times past, pushcart venders were considered to be somewhat unrespectable. Not anymore! As pedestrian malls and street corners become populated with more and more attractive carts with delicious health foods and unusual ethnic foods as well as traditional favorites, many people have come to rely on them for a quick snack or inexpensive lunch.

There are lots of advantages to running a pushcart business. Because most of them operate only during peak daytime hours, you have lots of time to devote to other activities. Utility bills are almost nonexistent for most pushcart foodcrafters, and many venders enjoy watching and interacting with the crowds of shop- pers. There are disadvantages too, of course. Rainy or freezing weather can ruin your mood and put a damper on profits, and the lack of space to move around in can be frustrating for some.

Starting Out

Getting into the pushcart business requires only minimal for- malities. A good product, a good location, some type of cart, and the proper licenses are the only real essentials. Because pushcarts sell directly to the public from a central location, they have some of the same licensing requirements as restaurants. In addition, they may be regulated by city or business commissions, which decide where they can park, what they can sell, and the hours they can operate. Pushcarts usually have specific areas in which they are allowed to operate, and the number of carts on a given block is usually limited. In some cities, carts must be serviced by an ap- proved commissary that packages the food to be sold (popcorn is usually an exception) and the carts must meet local health and sanitary standards. To find out the legal requirements in your area, contact your health department, state restaurant licensing authority, and zoning department.

Start-up Costs

In 1982, Denver pushcart venders reported an average investment of $3,000 for their carts, supplies, and licenses. You can reduce the cost by building the cart yourself, but again, be sure it meets local health standards.

At the other extreme you can go all out with a top-of-the-line cart. Patrick Kitowski, owner of a popcorn and peanut stand in Boulder, Colorado, contracted the manufacture of his elegant vending wagon, complete with oak trim and emerald green decor, for about $3,500. A few months later, food fair goers were snatching up the rights to similar wagons for $20,000.

The Profit Picture

Profits from pushcart vending largely depend on the nature of your product and the location of your cart, as well as the season of the year. An average day's sales in Boulder, Colorado in 1982 ran about $150, with a good day bringing in over $300 for some. With low overhead and minimal supply costs, most of that is profit, but pushcart vending will never make you rich. If you're planning on making your primary income from pushcart vending, you'll probably need to place several carts around town.

For more information about retail food businesses, refer to the retail section in the Specialty Foodcrafting chapter.

THE WRITING COOK

Can you write as well as you cook? If so, there are many ways to satisfy both career itches. Newspaper food columnists, restaurant and food critics, magazine food writers, and cookbook authors all profit from their double talents, and you can too.

Newspaper Columnists and Magazine Writers

If you would like to write for newspapers or magazines, start with your own best recipes. Anyone can copy old standards from the Betty Crocker Cookbook, but originality is the key for your success. After you've tested and retested each original recipe, write a few articles, each revolving around a different recipe or group of recipes. Remember that your editors will be judging you not only on your recipes but on your writing style as well. It should be a fresh and original style, supplementing the basic how-to information with interesting anecdotes, ideas for compatible dishes and serving and storage suggestions. Then visit you local editors or send your articles off to the appropriate magazines, along with information about yourself and a brief description of other articles that can be expected. Your chances with large publications are better, of course, if you've been published before. Starting out with a new magazine or your hometown newspaper may give you the edge you need for future publication or syndication in larger papers. Earnings, too, depend on your experience and the size of the paper or magazine. Expect them to provide a secondary income at best until you are fully established as a food writer.

Food and Restaurant Critic

Food and restaurant critics have to be especially knowledgeable about food, and not just about one type of cuisine. Your detailed descriptions and critiques must reflect a broad understanding of the finer points of food preparation and appreciation. Read up on new foods and gourmet trends in trade journals, national food magazines, and cookbooks, analyze the writings of other food critics, and practice rewriting their articles in your own style. Then, visit area restaurants and try out new foods, writing several critiques in the style that best fits each publication you would like to write for. Send them to the appropriate editor along with a current resume and information about any other article ideas you have. Competition in this business is tough, but once you've established yourself as an influential food critic, you've got a very enviable career ahead for yourself.

Cookbook Author

Literally hundreds of cookbooks are published every year in the United States. With the growing interest in microwave cooking, health and ethnic foods, quick meals and gourmet foods, the field is wide open for new recipes and fresh ideas. With a careful selection of your own tested recipes, a unique approach of some sort, and a good writing style, you can cash in on the growth in cookbook sales and build a rewarding career.

To begin with, you'll have to test and retest your recipes. You should ask friends in other parts of the country to try them in their own kitchens—a recipe that works well at sea level may literally flop at high altitudes. Testing a lot of recipes can run into a fair amount of money, so be prepared to make an early investment in your cookbook project. Unless you're an established author, most publishing houses will refuse to reimburse you for your research expenses.

Next, write sample chapters. Information about the background of a particular food makes interesting reading, and helps readers categorize it as part of an overall cuisine. Nika Hazelton, author of more than 22 cookbooks, includes information about the individual recipe, the appearance of the dish after cooking, its flavor, and a little history about it. By providing this background information, she helps her readers plan for complementary dishes and saves them the worry of ending up with a dish that might clash with family tastes.

Next you should outline the remaining chapters in detail, including sample recipes and the number of pages you expect the book to be. Submit it to one publisher at a time, always retaining your original copy for safekeeping. Don't get discouraged if you're turned down several times—different publishers are looking for different things, and sooner or later a good cookbook will find an appropriate publishing house.

One thing you should note is that a single cookbook will not make you rich. Cookbook writing is immensely time consuming, and profits are usually only mediocre. According to Nika, volume is what counts. Still, writing one excellent book can set you up to write others. There are other rewards, too. Widely known authors get deferential treatment from the public, and have an inroad to a variety of other food-related careers. If you love to write and you love to cook, writing a cookbook may be a satisfying combination of your talents.

MEDIA CHEFS

Do you dream of fame and fortune? Working as a television or radio chef can satisfy your craving for public attention and provide a good secondary income. With the tremendous growth of interest in gourmet cooking, more and more media stations are including cooking shows in their regular programming. Good cooks around the country are measuring, mixing, sauteeing and baking everything from macrobiotic meals to flambes in five- to fifteen-minute programs.

What does it take to become a media chef? According to Peter Kump, a cooking teacher and chef on two New York cable TV shows, the same things that make a good cooking teacher make a good media chef, including a thorough knowledge of the subject, attention to detail, and a pleasing personality. In addition, media chefs must audition for their parts just like any other actor or actress. "In the auditions, Peter says, "they'll often give you directions [just] to see if you can take directions, [and see] if you can change, modify." As with any teaching profession, he warns that theatrics and flamboyance take second place to a real concern for the students, a quality that is appreciated even when transmitted over radio and television.

Good teaching is impossible without good preparation, and with media chefs that's especially true because of the short time alloted their segments on most shows. Before you barge into the nearest media station, mixing bowls and spatulas in hand, note these suggestions that will make your audition easier and improve you chances of success.

• You won't have time to cook an entire dish on most shows. To conserve time, premeasure your ingredients and prepare examples of the dish in several different stages, including the completed dish. Save the highlights of your show for cooking techniques that may be unfamiliar to watchers, information about the dish, its uses and suggested complementary dishes.

• Practice, practice, practice! If you're great in front of an audience, you have a bigger chance of getting the job, and practice can improve the odds. Know the exact sequence of events you wish to follow and have a general outline prepared for your explanations but allow plenty of room for ad-libbing. Watch yourself in front of a mirror. Do you find yourself turning away from the camera (or mirror)? Are you smiling? Are you relaxed? Sure of yourself? Practice in front of neighbors, family members, and cooking class students if you already teach. Get their opinions, then refine and polish your presentation. If you need still more instruction, take a drama or speech class at a local community college or free school. Either can help give you the experience you need to work in front of a group of people.

• Take note of your appearance. Because you'll be on camera for television, or auditioning live for a radio show, how you look can be as important as what you do. Remember that cameras can make you look 10-15 pounds heavier, and other problems may also be accentuated.

• Talk to other media personalities, asking for tips on auditions and presentation. Many will be willing to help you and may be able to suggest a few television or radio stations looking for chefs.

Chapter 8
Financing Your Business

Once you start thinking about owning your own foodcrafting business, you'll have to think about financing. If you're like most people, the prospect of talking to bankers, setting up books, preparing tax returns, and making enough money to keep afloat may seem intimidating. And you're probably justified in being wary. You've been told the disheartening facts by friends, relatives, and the news media—nine out of ten new businesses fail before their fifth year; more businesses declared bankruptcy in 1982 than in any year since the depression (and experts predict that number will continue to rise); large corporations as well as small companies are being forced to merge together or shut their doors completely as America's economy falters.

If you're smart, you'll pay attention to the statistics because they're saying something you can't afford to ignore: a good idea is no longer enough to make a business profitable. Sound business practices, good management, and a great deal of planning and foresight are necessary for success, and these characteristics should be evident in your business well before you cater your first party or open the doors of your carry-out shop.

This chapter will give you general guidelines on how to get your business venture financed. But please note: there are dozens of books available which go into much greater detail on the financial aspects of running a business. This chapter isn't meant to cover everything, but only to serve as a general guide. Before you start *any* business, you should think about consulting an accountant, lawyer, and any experts who can give you advice on your specific foodcrafting business.

One of the best things about foodcrafting businesses is that many of them can be started on a shoestring. For the price of a few ingredients, a license or two and some advertising, you have a mailorder business or your own cooking school. Or, by investing in some flour and brown sugar and enough gasoline to get you to neighborhood stores, you can share your "decadently delicious" cookies with an entire city and make a tidy profit.

Sooner or later though, you'll probably need more money. Whether for the initial start-up costs, expansion funds, or just to carry you through a short-term cash crunch, financing is usually essential, and that means planning for it well in advance of your actual need for it. It is always much easier to arrange a loan when you don't need one than when you do need one, as paradoxical as that may seem.

WHERE TO GET THE MONEY YOU NEED

Your very best option for financing is, of course, your own savings. If you've saved enough over the years to completely finance your start-up and later expansion, consider yourself lucky indeed. The advantages to this approach are obvious: by using your own money, you avoid monthly loan and interest payments, and you retain complete control over the business—no one can tell you how to make your decisions.

But if you're like most people, you just don't have that kind of money to start with. If you're convinced, though, that your business will succeed and you've done the research to back up your business plan, there are several options which may be open to you.

Family and Friends

When Robert and Stacey Bremers decided to open a specialty food store in Boulder, Colorado, their parents jointly invested about $40,000. That opened the doors, but the money was soon used for inventory and operating costs, and the Bremers had to ask their parents for additional funds. They were lucky: by 1982 the loan had been fully repaid and Essential Ingredients was grossing about $250,000.

Ben Strohecker started his mail-order gourmet candy business on a shoestring and made it into a good part-time business. But when it came time to expand, Ben's loan proposal was turned down by the SBA, banks, and venture capitalists. It took the faith of eight friends, each investing $2,000, to keep the business going long enough for it to grow to its current success (now grossing about $150,000). "One of them set it up," he recalled. "He said, 'You call these four names, and I'll call the following four names, and we'll meet at your place on Thursday night. I protested that they were my friends and I didn't want to get my friends involved, but he assured me that they were all big boys and to shut up and do as I was told. And they each gave me $2,000. . . .'"

Family and friends have been the salvation of many a business—because they know and trust the owner, they tend to have more faith in the potential of the business than a bank would and they are often more lenient with repayment. There is risk in any new business, however, and the truth is that your family or friends could end up losing their money. For that reason, many people advise against borrowing from family and friends. If you're the type of person who would rather risk the money of a stranger than of the people you love, you're better off looking at other options.

Partners

Many businesses that couldn't otherwise have gotten off the ground or found financing necessary for expansion have been saved by selling a part of the business to a partner. Partnerships are easy to arrange legally, and there are advantages to having other people involved in your business who have the same dedication and interest in the venture's success as you do. But there are disadvantages too, and they should be seriously considered before you sign the papers turning over part ownership of your business. You'll probably be working with your partner from eight to twelve or more hours a day, so it's imperative that your personalities and business styles be compatible. And you'll have to agree on the goals of your business: if your partner wants to franchise your catering business in 30 states and you want to focus entirely on the local market, you've got the beginnings of a rocky relationship. In fact, the whole concept of business partnerships is similar to marriage, as Stacey Bremers pointed out:

"You have your conflicts and your ups and downs," she added, "and you just constantly have to be feeding back to each other. Otherwise problems arise—personality conflicts." And, she said, the dissolution of a partnership can be as traumatic as a divorce, and as expensive.

Venture Capitalists

Some individuals, groups and companies specialize in start-up business investments by supplying "venture" capital in return for part ownership of the new company. The Small Business Administration (SBA) regulates and licenses privately owned Small Business Investment Companies (SBICs) whose main purpose is to invest in new businesses. They sometimes loan money more readily than banks to companies which are not able to provide adequate collateral. Because these are "for profit" companies, they are usually unwilling to invest any amount in a company which fails to meet their investment criteria.

Minority Enterprise Small Business Investment Companies (MESBIC) are licensed by the SBA to assist economically or socially disadvantaged business owners. Under certain circumstances Caucasian women qualify for this special assistance.

Other venture capitalists include "silent" partners who invest money but leave management decisions to you, and institutions which reserve special funds for higher-risk investments. To find venture capitalists in your area, talk with your banker, attorney, friends, and other business owners.

Insurance Companies

Don't overlook your life insurance policy as a source of potential cash. If you've been making payments for three or more years, your policy may have accumulated a substantial cash value which will be refunded to you if you cash in the policy or against which you may borrow instead of cashing in the policy. If you borrow money from your insurance company, you will find that the interest rate is probably much lower than bank interest rates, and your policy will remain in effect during the loan repayment period.

Banks

The high interest rates of the last several years have made bank loans more expensive and harder to get, especially for new and untested businesses. But don't be discouraged before you try. Banks are in business to make money, including money from interest on loans. Providing you have a professional proposal and a sound business plan, they may just as well loan money to you as to anyone else.

HOW TO GET A BANK LOAN

You'll probably have to present your business proposal to a number of different banks, and the best place to start is with the one that handles your personal account. Your banking record and acquaintance with the bank's officers can definitely work to your advantage. If you're turned down by your own bank, ask for personal references from any of the officers who know you and are sympathetic to your business venture. Just because the bank turned you down doesn't mean that its officers won't put in a good word for you elsewhere.

Small, progressive banks are much more likely to lend you

money for your new business than are larger, more conservative ones, so concentrate your efforts on them. A bank's advertising style and content and your own conversations with its officers will help you determine how progressive it is.

Industrial banks are another source of business capital, but they usually charge higher interest rates than other banks. It may be worth your while to check with them, however, as well as savings and loan institutions, because their loan budgets are usually substantial and they're experienced in dealing with business start-ups.

Meeting With Bankers

If you've never talked with a loan officer before, you may find yourself being a little intimidated. And, if the truth is told, some bankers take advantage of the near-universal nervousness of loan applicants, and they can make your few minutes with them humbling indeed. It may help you to remember that bankers are NOT infallible—business start-ups that are repeatedly denied bank loans often go on to become quite successful. You have every right to expect polite and courteous treatment, and you can help insure that for yourself by preparing a good proposal and arriving for your appointment with a positive, determined attitude. If nothing else, your banker will respect your demeanor and just may be sufficiently impressed to give you the loan.

It's important to establish a good working relationship with your loan officer. To do that, make sure all loan payments (business and personal) are made on time and keep your loan officer informed of developments in your business. You may find that your loan officer is an excellent source of helpful financial advice, and by seeking his opinions you'll show him that you take your business very seriously. If you treat your banker with respect and friendliness, he will know that your customers are treated the same way, and that can make a difference the next time you need financing.

Most of all, remember that bankers are people too. Although they deal with figures and percentages all day, most of them will tell you that their better loan judgments are at least partly based on "gut" feelings about the business owner and his capabilities, and that the human factor does play a significant role in their loan decisions.

How To Ask for a Loan

So what is going through the banker's mind while you're pouring out your dreams and business plans to him? He's judging your character, your sincerity, your ability to repay a loan, and your credit-worthiness in general. If you already know the banker, you're one step ahead because he already knows something about your background. But whether or not you're friends with your banker, there are certain things you'll need to prove about yourself and your business. Stop and imagine yourself in your prospective lender's shoes for a moment, and honestly assess the answers you can give to the questions he'll be asking himself about you:

• What is your general character? Are you trustworthy? Are you honest in your business dealings? Do you have a history of making loan payments on time? Is your personal account free of returned checks and overextended credit limits? Do you keep appointments, or at least call when you're going to be unavoidably late? Can you be trusted to manage a large sum of money judiciously, or are you likely to spend the funds frivolously? What is it about you that will make him sure you can, and will, repay the loan?

• Do you need a short-term or long-term loan? What will the money be used for? Your planned use of the money will largely determine the amount of time you have to repay the loan.

• How will you repay the loan? Can you show a reasonable prediction of how the business will generate enough money for monthly payments?

• How will the loan be secured? Do you personally have

enough collateral, or do you have the guaranty of a financially solvent person so that the repayment of the loan is insured in case of business failure?

• What is the current state of the economy? Are the prospects for business success good? Will your particular business succeed in this area? Can you prove it?

• If you've been in business for awhile, can you show that it's profitable and growing? Are your records in good condition? Do you pay your bills on time? Are you good at collecting from customers? Are your taxes paid on time? Do you have adequate insurance? Are you in good standing with government regulatory authorities? What is the condition of your equipment and the building from which you run your business?

To answer all of these questions to the satisfaction of a banker, it's important that you have the necessary financial information at hand. A good loan officer won't even consider your loan request unless it's presented in the form of a professional proposal that includes all the information necessary for an intelligent decision. So get yourself a good accountant or financial consultant and put together the following information, making sure it is concise, readable, neat and accurate.

• *Current Financial Statement.* This will include a list of all of your assets and liabilities. A personal financial statement is mandatory, and if you've been operating your business for awhile you'll need a business financial statement as well.

• *Current Balance Sheet.* Like a snapshot of your account ledger, a balance sheet will show your current cash positions and must include a listing of business assets and liabilities. (If you're seeking a loan for start-up costs, separate lists of business and personal assets and liabilities will suffice.) Assets include equipment, inventory, equity, accounts receivable, and anything else which you can convert into cash. Liabilities include accounts payable, rent or mortgage payments due, taxes, insurance, salaries and other payments that must be made. On a balance sheet, your assets and liabilities will always be equal.

• *Profit and Loss Statement.* This details your earnings for a period of time (usually a year, or however long you've been in operation) by showing a series of monthly balance sheets. It should include the name of suppliers and the amount of money paid to each. Expenditures will be categorized by type (inventory, equipment service, rent, etc.). Your accountant or bookkeeper can help you with this.

• *Cash Flow Projection.* A forecast of the money you anticipate receiving and spending over a period of time (usually a year), the cash flow projection is one of your most important planning tools. It should be realistic. Projections of phenomenal growth may look good on paper, but will only serve to make your banker suspicious. In general it's a good idea to be conservative with your projected profit figures and generous with your expenditure figures. Graphs or any other diagrams that will help chart your expenses, income and predicted break-even point should be included here.

• *History of Your Company.* If you've been in business for awhile, tell your banker about it! How did you get the idea for the business? How did you start? Are there other businesses like yours that have been successful? What do your customers or clients say about it? (The inclusion of written testimonials from satisfied customers can definitely help.) What are some of the major problems you've faced? How did you handle them? Don't be afraid to talk about problems, there's not a business in existance that hasn't had some. Your ability to resolve them will show the banker your resourcefulness and willingness to persevere.

• *Your Capital Needs.* Why do you need a loan? What do you plan to do with the money? If you're planning to buy major pieces of equipment, include detailed descriptions with prices included. Brochures with the equipment pictured can be helpful, but be sure to include the reasons your business requires the equipment. If you need the loan to cover operating expenses, show how the money will be spent. Include the cost of rent, salaries, utilities, and other expenses, and document the figures by providing previous receipts and/or future cost projections from the supplier company.

• *Personal References.* At least three, and preferably five or more written references should be obtained from friends, business acquaintances, or companies with which you've dealt in the past. The person writing the letter should have personally known you for at least one year. The more respect the person commands in your community, of course, the more helpful the letter will be. Be sure that the letters include information about your general character traits and the person's judgment of your ability to succeed in your particular business.

Once your banker has had time to review your proposal, you're ready to sit down and discuss the type of loan you need, the security you'll provide, and repayment terms. These considerations are usually partially covered during the initial interview, but final decisions should be made only after you've explored all the options for your loan with your banker.

Types of Bank Loans

The type of loan you need depends on how you plan to spend the money and how you'll pay it back. Most banks will require a monthly installment and will require penalty payments if you go beyond the payment due date. Your loan may be structured with a fixed rate of interest or an adjustable interest rate, and without predicting the course of future interest rates, it's impossible to say which would be better for you. Loans structured with large "balloon" payments at the end should be avoided unless you're absolutely conviced your cash picture will allow payment of a lump sum at the specified date. If your business is seasonal, you may want to structure higher payments during prosperous months and lower, more manageable payments during the lean times.

If your business is running smoothly but you need some cash to tide you through a slow season, a short-term loan will serve the purpose. Repayment terms can run from 30 days to a year. Your banker will expect the money to be repaid as soon as it has served the purpose for which it was borrowed. If you used the money to buy inventory, the proceeds from the sale of the inventory will probably be available long before a year is up, but if you use the money for operating expenses, your bank is likely to be a bit more lenient about the due date for repayment. In general, loans used for purchases of liquid assets will have shorter due dates than money used for equipment purchase or operating expenses.

There are really two types of long-term loans: those that will be repaid in one to five years and those that will require longer than five years to repay. For your purposes, the former type will probably do (unless you plan to purchase extremely expensive equipment, the bank will probably want its money back within two to three years). Unlike short-term loans, long-term loans almost always require an equal or greater amount of collateral or security and are expected to be repaid in monthly installments from your earnings.

SECURITY

The recent increase in business bankruptcies has made it more difficult than ever to acquire unsecured loans. In fact, most banks won't consider a long-term loan proposal from a new business without impressive collateral or security, although short-term loans can sometimes be obtained on the basis of a good credit record alone. In your loan proposal, you'll include a list of personal and business assets which can be used as collateral. These assets may include real estate, stocks and bonds, accounts receivables, savings accounts, life insurance policies, mutual funds or money market funds, trust accounts, or saleable personal property. Personal guarantors, lease assignments, chattel mortgages, and loan endorsers or co-makers are other forms of security for a loan.

Real Estate

Your home should be used as loan collateral only as a final resort—the risk of your business failing is bad enough without the added risk of losing the roof over your head. Other real estate which you may own can provide substantial collateral for your business loan. If you own real property which draws rent, try pledging rent receipts first before offering the entire property as collateral.

Stocks and Bonds

Because the stock market is unpredictable, banks lend only about 75 percent of the market value of most blue chip stocks. Federal and municipal bonds are considered more conservative, and you may get 90 percent of their market value (but if the market drops, you may be required to supply additional security).

Accounts Receivable

If you have significant outstanding payments due your business and can document it to the satisfaction of your bank, you may be able to pledge the forthcoming payments as loan security. The bank may allow you to make the payments or may go directly to your customers for payment. (As the owner/operator of a small foodcrafting business, you should generally avoid getting into a position where you are owed large sums of money by customers or clients, but you may find that large accounts draw out their payments from one to three months. In that case, the money they owe you is good security for a short-term loan.)

Savings Accounts

Instead of withdrawing the money in your personal or business savings account, you may want to use the account as security for a loan. You'll be paying a higher interest rate on the money that you borrow than you're receiving for your savings, but some people have no other options for establishing credit and believe the expense is justified.

Life Insurance Policies

Before borrowing from a bank against the cash value of your life insurance policy, find out what interest rate your insurance company is charging for similar loans. You might be able to save money with your insurance company's (generally lower) interest rate, but be sure to check on the effect, if any, this would have on the protection of your beneficiary during the repayment term.

Personal Property

Banks may also lend you money for the market value of your car, boat, household items, jewelry, or other personal property. Any such items used as security must be fully owned by you, and you would be responsible for obtaining proof of their current market value.

Guarantors, Endorsers, and Co-makers

If you lack adequate security for the loan you can seek the help of another person (usually a friend or relative) who is willing to become responsible for the loan in the event you can't repay it. A complete financial statement is usually required from such a person, and he may be asked to supply collateral. There are three ways another person can help you secure a loan: by acting as a personal guarantor, an endorser, or a co-maker. Endorsers and personal guarantors essentially agree to pay the entire note if the original borrower fails to do so, and many lenders require that corporate officers act as personal guarantors for the business. A co-maker usually acts as a partner in the business, and the bank may collect from either party, or may collect an equal amount from each party.

Chattel Mortgages

If the purpose of your proposed loan is to finance equipment, the bank may offer to lend you the money and assume a lien on the equipment. In that case, only the equipment reverts to the bank if you can't make payments. However, banks will rarely lend you the full amount which you pay for your equipment without additional security. Instead, they will determine the present and projected future market value of the equipment and the amount of time it will probably take to sell it, and lend you some percentage of the total cost. Unfortunately, that percentage can run as low as 10 percent of the price you pay for the equipment and, in the case of kitchen equipment, will rarely run as high as 50 percent.

In deciding on the type of collateral you want to use for a loan, you'll naturally be limited by the kind of material and intangible assets you own. Most banks will consider a combination of various types of security, but to protect themselves they usually require you to pledge a great deal more than you're borrowing. It can be risky to tie up your savings account, home, car, and household possessions, so be sure you've left yourself enough leeway in case your business doesn't do as well as you expect it to.

SOME TIPS ON DEALING WITH BANKERS

Bankers, like most other people, are impressed by those who are positive, organized, neat in appearance, and who have the intelligence and foresight to make a business idea succeed. So work up your courage, put on your best business clothes, and sell your banker on yourself and your ability to do the job. It may help you to be convincing if you remember that other people like your business idea and can vouch for your level of responsibility.

Don't forget that your banker can be an excellent reference for you once he gets to know you and your business. Invite him to visit a cooking class, or offer to cater the bank's Christmas party. Bankers tend to know a lot of influential people in their community, and the right word at the right time from your banker could mean substantial new business for you.

Some people forget that bankers can also provide them with financial consultation and advice. In fact, many bankers are flattered when customers respect their opinions enough to seek them out. They know what has worked for other companies, and may be able to give you some new ideas about money management. They can also give you the names of good accountants, attorneys, and other professionals whose help you may need, and they can be a good reference for other business transactions. Cultivate your banker's respect and friendship, and you'll have a valuable ally in times of need.

GOVERNMENT ASSISTANCE: THE SBA

The Small Business Administration was created to encourage the development and growth of independently owned companies through financial assistance, management assistance and education. Most major cities have SBA offices, and each office houses a library of hundreds of free or low-cost pamphlets which can inform small business owners and managers about an amazing variety of business topics. In addition, the SBA offers management workshops and seminars, and special programs for minority businesspeople and socially and economically disadvantaged groups are scheduled.

For years, the SBA had a reputation for granting low-interest loans to almost any applicant who had an idea and a little business acumen. Today, however, you'll hear plenty of complaints about the bureaucratic red tape involved in getting an SBA loan and the severly limited funds available to businesses through the agency. And, the success of loan applications often appears to be based more on the whim of the individual SBA loan officer and his superiors than on the merit of the particular application. But if you've got the time, the motivation and the patience to apply, your efforts might be rewarded with the money you need at an attractive rate of interest.

Types of SBA Assistance

The SBA provides two types of financial assistance: direct loans and guarantees for bank loans. A direct loan is designed to finance up to 80 percent of your start-up costs and usually requires proof that you've invested some of your own money. The typical payback period is five to eight years. Your application must include proof that your loan proposal has been denied by at least two banks if you live in a city of 200,000 or more, and the SBA may impose certain limits or restrictions on how you operate your business.

Under the "Loan Guarantee Plan," the SBA will guarantee 90 percent of a bank loan. This is, by far, the most common type of SBA assistance, but it is clearly less desirable because it means paying the higher bank interest rates.

Special assistance programs are offered for expanding businesses, handicapped and minority businesses, and existing businesses with special problems. The National Women's Business Ownership Campaign, founded by the SBA in 1977, has been especially effective in helping women to begin and expand their own businesses, and the Minority Small Business and Capital Ownership Development Program gives technical, financial, and management assistance to minority women.

SBA loans can be a new businesses' best option for start-up money, but the length of time required to process and approve the loan can be extremely discouraging. In addition, the SBA is severely limited in funds, and about 75 percent of the money loaned out goes to existing and expanding companies that have a proven track record.

If you know of a banker that's willing to work with you in applying for an SBA guaranteed loan, ask him for assistance with your proposal, and encourage him to submit the application. Usually the SBA will deal directly through him, and his past experience with the program will be extremely helpful to you.

Some Final Words

It's true that the American economy isn't as healthy as it once was, and that more and more businesses are declaring bankruptcy or selling out to their competition as money tightens. But even in the worst of times, good ideas and good products that are needed and wanted by their markets have provided the foundation for many a booming business. And most of the foodcrafters we interviewed had very encouraging comments about the ability of their business to weather hard economic times.

As Ben Strohecker of Harbor Sweets put it, "I don't think there's ever a bad time to go into this business. It's a big country. If a little cottage industry is something you really believe the consumer has a need for, and you're committed to it, I don't care what the economic times are—you'll be successful!"

Appendix A

SOURCES OF ADDITIONAL INFORMATION

Organizations

The Foodcrafters' Guild, 6003 North 51st Street, P.O. Box 2193, Boulder, CO 80306. The Guild is "a clearinghouse of ideas, resources and information for profitable foodcrafting." Send your name and address for information on the Guild newsletter, books, cassette tapes and other resources.

National Association for the Specialty Food Trade, Inc. (NASFT), 1270 Ave. of the Americas, New York, NY 10020. Membership in NASFT is somewhat expensive ($200 to $400 a year) but is necessary if you want to exhibit at their Fancy Food & Confection shows, which can be well worthwhile.

Books

Finance

How to Finance Your Small Business With Government Money: SBA Loans. Rick Stephan Hayes and John Cotton Howell; John Wiley & Sons; 1980 ($14.95)

The Small Business Guide to Borrowing Money, by Richard L. Rubin and Philip Goldberg. McGraw-Hill Book Co., New York, 1980.

Foodcrafting

How to Run a Successful Specialty Food Store, by Douglass L. Brownstone. New York: John Wiley & Sons, Inc. 1978.

Cater From Your Kitchen, by Marjorie Blanchard. Bobbs-Merrill Company, Inc., Indianapolis, Indiana.

General

Small Business Management by William D. Hailes, Jr. and Raymond T. Hubbard. New York: Van Nostrand, 1977.

Small-Time Operator by Bernard Kamoroff, C.P.A., Bell Springs Publishing Co., P.O. Box 322, Laytonville, CA 95454

Legal

The Small Business Legal Advisor, by William A. Hancock. McGraw-Hill, 1982.

Mail Order

Direct Marketing, by Edward L. Nash. McGraw-Hill Book Company, New York. (hardcover, $24.95)

How to Start and Operate a Mail-Order Business, by Julian L. Simon. New York, McGraw-Hill. (hardcover, $19.95)

Mail Order!, by Eugene M. Schwartz. Boardroom Books, Box 1026, Millburn, NJ 07041

Mail-Order Moonlighting by Cecil C. Hoge, Sr. Ten Speed Press, P.O. Box 7123, Berkeley, CA 94707. Softcover, $7.95.

Time Management

Advanced Learning Systems (cassette tapes), 13906 Ventura Blvd., Sherman Oaks, CA 91423

Success Books (cassette tapes and books), Box 134, Old Bethpage, NY 11804

Women

A Directory of Federal Government Business Assistance Programs for Women. Free from Superintendent of Documents, U.S. Government Printing Office, Washington, DC 20402

Women and the SBA and *Women's Handbook: How the SBA Can Help You Go Into Business.* Both free from your local SBA office.

The Woman's Guide to Starting a Business, by Claudia Jessup and Genie Hipps. New York: Holt, Rinehart and Winston, 1979 ($6.95)

Appendix B

Small Business Administration (SBA) Field Offices:

Agana, GU
Albany, NY
Albuquerque, NM
Anchorage, AK
Atlanta, GA
Augusta, ME
Baltimore, MD
Biloxi, MS
Birmingham, AL
Boise, ID
Boston, MA
Buffalo, NY
Camden, NJ
Casper, WY
Charleston, WV
Charlotte, NC
Chicago, IL

Cincinnati, OH
Columbia, SC
Columbus, OH
Concord, NH
Coral Gables, FL
Corpus Christi, TX
Dallas, TX
Denver, CO
Des Moines, IA
Detroit, MI
Eau Claire, WI
Elmira, NY
El Paso, TX
Fairbanks, AK
Fargo, ND
Fresno, CA
Knoxville, TN

Las Vegas, NV
Little Rock, AR
Louisville, KY
Lubbock, TX
Madison, WI
Marquette, MI
Marshall, TX
Melville, NY
Memphis, TN
Milwaukee, WI
Minneapolis, MN
Montpelier, VT
Nashville, TN
Newark, NJ
New Orleans, LA
New York, NY
Oklahoma City, OK
Omaha, NB
Philadelphia, PA
Phoenix, AZ
Pittsburgh, PA
Portland, OR
Providence, RI
Rapid City, SD
Reno, NV
Richmond, VA
Rochester, NY
St. Louis, MO
St. Thomas, VI
Sacramento, CA

Salt Lake City, UT
San Antonio, TX
San Diego, CA
Greenville, NC
Harlingen, TX
Harrisburg, PA
Hartford, CT
Hato Rey, PR
Helena, MT
Holyoke, MA
Honolulu, HI
Houston, TX
Indianapolis, IN
Jackson, MS
Jacksonville, FL
Kansas City, MO
San Francisco, CA
Seattle, WA
Shreveport, LA
Sioux Falls, SD
Spokane, WA
Springfield, IL
Syracuse, NY
Tampa, FL
Washington, DC
West Palm Beach, FL
Wichita, KS
Wilkes-Barre, PA
Wilmington, DE